MORE GREAT
CAT STORIES

MORE GREAT CAT STORIES

Incredible Tales About Exceptional Cats

ROXANNE WILLEMS SNOPEK

VICTORIA · VANCOUVER · CALGARY

Heritage House Publishing Company Ltd.
www.heritagehouse.ca

Library and Archives Canada Cataloguing in Publication

Snopek, Roxanne Willems
   More great cat stories: incredible tales about exceptional cats /
Roxanne Willems Snopek. — 1st Heritage House ed.

(Amazing stories)
ISBN 978-1-894974-55-4

   1. Cats—Canada—Anecdotes. 2. Cat owners—Canada—Anecdotes.
I. Title. II. Series.

SF445.5.S66 2008   636.8'0887   C2008-905642-6

Also available in e-pub format, ISBN 978-1-926613-71-0

Edited by Deborah Lawson and Margaret Sadler.
Proofread by Lesley Reynolds.
Cover design by Chyla Cardinal. Interior design by Frances Hunter.
Cover photo by Mert Kanar/iStockphoto. Interior photos by Alexandria Tiffinger, page 27; Cathie Newman, page 48; Roxanne Willems Snopek, page 112; Stephanie Snopek, page 127.

MIX
Paper from
responsible sources
FSC
www.fsc.org   FSC™ C016245

The interior of this book was produced using 100% post-consumer recycled paper, processed chlorine free and printed with vegetable-based inks.

Heritage House acknowledges the financial support for its publishing program from the Government of Canada through the Canada Book Fund (CBF), Canada Council for the Arts and the province of British Columbia through the British Columbia Arts Council and the Book Publishing Tax Credit.

Canada Council
for the Arts
Conseil des Arts
du Canada

BRITISH COLUMBIA
ARTS COUNCIL

13 12 11 10   2 3 4 5
Printed in Canada

Contents

Prologue

IT WAS THE SPRING OF 1977 and my greatest wish was about to come true. Cinders, my very own cat, was going to have kittens! Each day I feverishly rushed through my schoolwork, eager for the dismissal bell to ring and the bus to deposit me back at home. I raced along the driveway, dropped my bags and jacket, and went to check on her. In all my 14 years, nothing was as thrilling as the anticipation of "cat grandmotherhood." I thought I might burst with excitement before the event actually took place.

Throughout my childhood, I had always loved cats and wished for one with all my heart. Now, not only did I have my own cat, but she was going to become a mother! It just didn't get any better than that.

When the day finally arrived, I tiptoed over to the carefully prepared box in the corner of my bedroom, my heart in my throat. To my surprise, the box was empty. I scanned the room. Nothing. I looked in the closets, under the beds, beneath the stairs. But the mother-to-be was nowhere to be found.

As on most farmyards in the area, half-wild cats skulked on the periphery of human activity, ever wary of coming too near the domestic inhabitants. They were twitchy, ill-fed things, riddled with disease and parasites, here one day and gone the next. Cinders, however, was different. She was cared for and loved. Her kittens would be different, too, I vowed. After all, they were mine.

Tears of panic filled my eyes as I intensified my search. I'd kept Cinders confined to the house for the past few days and instructed my family not to let her out, for fear of predators who would have loved to come upon a nest of new kittens. But my precautions had been in vain. I scanned the outbuildings and barns, the corrals and haystacks, the wide-open fields beyond, knowing the hiding places outside were infinite.

I might never find her.

1

Calico Serendipity

"It is very lucky to have a cat of three colours come to your house." —TRADITIONAL PROVERB

CINDERS WAS NOT MY FIRST cat. When I was about five years old, my parents got a pair of kittens for my younger sister and me. Immediately upon their arrival in our home, Blacky and Spotty made tracks for the hidden spot behind the sofa and refused to come out. With two youngsters poking and prodding at them, their hissing and spitting were appropriate, possibly life-saving, reactions. But my sister and I were so disappointed; we wanted to play with our new pets. I realize now that the kittens were nearly feral (wild), or poorly socialized at best; they preferred to keep their distance and within a few months they'd both disappeared.

Shortly afterward, our family embarked on the first of several moves. And while my parents indulged my love for animals as much as they could, my insatiable need for four-legged companionship didn't mix well with the upheaval of boxes and moving vans. I took comfort in our dog Fluffy, a budgie named Sharpie, and what I suspect was a regular turnover of goldfish. A cat would have to wait.

But I could still read about cats. As I grew older, my parents faithfully turned me loose in the public library, where I invariably ended up in the pet section. I knew it blindfolded—cat breeds, cat care, cat training, feeding, grooming, showing—finding and reading all the books they had on my favourite subject. Before I was a teenager, I'd read about Colette's famous cats and knew about Hemingway's multi-toed felines. I could tell Persians from Himalayans, Burmese from Siamese, Manx from bobtails. I'd read that tortoiseshell cats were believed to be able to see into the future and could impart that gift to a lucky child in their household. Dreaming over the dusty stacks of books, I took flight into a world in which I was no longer a gawky, tongue-tied child, but a powerful seer, always accompanied by my faithful animal companions.

Even history came alive when the right details were included. I discovered I had something in common with the infamous Cardinal Richelieu, who lived in the time of the witch-hunts of the 1600s. The Cardinal was an ardent cat-lover, a fact inexplicably left out of my social studies textbook. Although cats were linked to witches by superstition, the Cardinal ignored this in deference to the 14 cats that lived in a special room next to his own bedroom. On his deathbed, the Cardinal made provision for all his cats, and their two attendants, in his will. Sadly, as soon as he died the soldiers of his Swiss Guard burned the poor creatures to death as vengeance for the many witches—and, by association, their cats—that Richelieu had put to death in his lifetime.

While my classmates discussed the legacies of great political leaders, I daydreamed about other more interesting things. Sir Winston Churchill, for instance, loved his cat Jock so much that he shared his bed and his meals with him. In fact, if Jock wasn't at the table Churchill would dispatch a servant to find him and wait to begin eating until the cat arrived. And the great humanitarian, Albert Schweitzer, who was left-handed, sometimes wrote with his right arm rather than disturb his beloved cat Sizi, who liked to sleep on his left arm. He chose poor penmanship and pins-and-needles when his numb arm was finally released, rather than disturb her rest.

Being at the age where children begin looking toward their future careers, I thought I might become a nurse one day. Imagine my delight to discover that Florence Nightingale was a great cat lover! Although she often complained that they messed up her papers, the comfort they must have brought her after long hours of difficult work apparently made up for it, because she owned more than 60 cats over the course of her life.

I spent a great deal of my childhood with my nose buried in books. I wasn't picky—I read everything I could get my hands on. Adventure stories, romance, mysteries, westerns, science fiction, fantasy. Animal stories were, of course, the best. *Black Beauty, Old Yeller, The Yearling, The Red Pony, The Incredible Journey, Hurry Home, Candy, Born Free* . . . the list goes on and on. Paul Gallico could only have written *Jenny*, one of the most beautiful and moving books ever written about a stray cat, out of a soul-deep feline connection. What a thrill to learn that authors such as Victor Hugo, Edgar Allan Poe, Mark Twain, and H.G. Wells were cat lovers, too.

History records a few famous cat haters, too. The beauty of Brahms' lullabies was forever tainted when I read that one of his favourite forms of relaxation was to sit at an open window and hunt neighbourhood cats with his bow and arrow. It goes to show, I thought, what happens when you spend too much time practising piano. Napoleon Bonaparte was supposedly once found nearly hysterical with fear, sweating and lunging wildly with his sword, all because a small kitten had entered the room.

Immersed as I was in cat lore, it didn't take the place of real, living felines, but I made do as best I could. I got to know all the neighbourhood strays and gave names to all the cats that earned their keep at my grandparents' farm: thin, unkempt, half-wild creatures that I coaxed and cajoled until they let me near enough to stroke them. Skittles and

Tansy and Periwinkle and others I've long since forgotten. But I still didn't have a cat of my own.

Finally, four moves later, as I was entering junior high school, we were ready to stay put. My parents purchased 80 acres of flat land filled with rocks, scrubby bushes, and poplar bluffs and made plans to build a house. After years of what felt like cramped city living, I had space to move and grow, fresh air to savour, and enough quiet to hear my own thoughts. I'd never liked urban living; I longed for wide-open spaces, birdsong, alfalfa-scented air, and silent, starry nights.

Construction started as soon as the snow melted in the spring, when furry crocuses covered the fields with their delicate mauve mirage. Leaves unfolded from the bushes and wildflowers sprang to life. Red-winged blackbirds called from the lilacs; crows and magpies scolded us from the tree-tops; bluebirds perched on the fence-posts and sang to us of happiness. It was an exhausting summer for my parents, but I was so excited about this move. This time, I knew, I could finally have a cat!

Her name was Nutmeg. She was a silky-coated calico, glossy black fur patched with orange and white, her face a perfect bisection of black and orange. She was beautiful. She slept in my bed at night and prowled the wilderness during the day.

That winter, icy winds and a heavy prairie snowfall put construction on hold until spring, so our family lived in the basement of our half-finished home. My parents, my sister and I, and now a younger brother as well, lived in two small bedrooms piled high with boxes that wouldn't be unpacked until the top half of our house materialized. Running water, plumbing, and electricity had been installed before winter hit, but it was still rough living by today's standards. I loved everything about it—except the bugs. Spiders crept along the open beams above my bed, moths fluttered around bare light-bulbs, and in my nightmares, dark things slithered and crawled beneath my bed.

Our house was eventually completed and life settled down. Other cats joined our family. Two males belonged to my sister: a big grey-and-white cat named Napoleon— wouldn't the little general just spin in his grave!—and a fluffy ginger tabby named Butternut. For my part, I had two pure white, blue-eyed cats, April and Honeydew, both of whom were afflicted with the lethal white gene that causes deafness. I loved them for their beauty, those great azure eyes sparkling in a sea of snowy fur. But I couldn't protect them from their disability and both of them were killed by cars they did not hear coming.

Then came Cinders. Unlike Nutmeg's clearly defined patches, Cinders' white and orange hairs were evenly dispersed throughout the black background, giving her the distinctive tortoiseshell coloration. Down her nose ran one thin, clear, white stripe. Her coat of ashes-and-soot was not as eye-catching as some of the more distinctive varieties of cats; in fact, she was actually rather plain. But as she grew, her fur became glossy and lush over lean, graceful muscles, and through her ordinary exterior sparkled a character of breathtaking beauty. She carried herself with an air of calm that spread and settled on anyone with whom she chose to share herself. And she chose to share herself with me.

The many fears and insecurities that arose during my tumultuous teen years were soothed by her peaceful purr and warmth. Looking into her eyes, I felt myself drift away from the troubles of the moment, carried off to someplace new, where I wasn't a shy, skinny bookworm with glasses and braces. When she sought me out and took pleasure in my company I felt that, to her, I was more than just a kid. I was a person, someone special.

In the spring of 1977, as Cinders' belly grew larger, my nightmare became real when a plague of forest tent caterpillars invaded central Saskatchewan. At first, as I walked down the driveway to meet the school bus, I tried to avoid stepping on them. But eventually I gave up the hopeless attempt, and instead began counting to see how many I would squash with each normal footstep. I quit counting at 100.

I'd never seen so many insects at one time and these filled me with a special kind of horror. They congregated in great seething clusters. They covered the highway in a slick, slimy film that could send incautious drivers skating into the ditch. Their inexorable masses slithered over the fields, eating everything green in sight. They clung to the sides of the house, falling onto unwary passersby. Clumps of poplars and trembling aspen were denuded overnight, and the green fields turned brown and crisp.

As the armies of tiny *Malacosoma disstria* marched over the land, I focussed on the impending birth. I made a bed for Cinders and her babies, a box thickly lined with newspapers and old towels. I showed her the box and she obligingly curled up in it, purring her appreciation. I lived in an agony of anticipation, barely able to concentrate on my classes. As the time approached for her kittens to be born—cats have a 63-day gestation period, as I knew from my earlier reading—I could focus on nothing else. Finally, after weeks of tormenting slowness, the day had arrived.

And now she was gone.

I searched high and low for her, in all the nooks and crannies inside and out, but Cinders was nowhere to be found. I squeamishly kept away from the low-lying bushes near the house; the great masses of caterpillars were heaviest there. But finally, all other possibilities exhausted, I squatted down for a look. There, protected on all sides by a dense tangle of twigs and branches, lay Cinders, curled around four newborn kittens. She looked up at me and chirped a greeting. About a foot above her, a horde of caterpillars approximately the size of a soccer-ball writhed and squirmed. Cinders gently detached herself from her infants, picked up one in her jaws and walked toward me.

"That's my girl," I said, reaching for her. But she scooted

under my hands and ran toward the house. At the door, she stopped, set down her baby, and looked over her shoulder at me. As soon as I opened the door, she repositioned her kitten between her jaws and trotted into the house, straight to the bed I'd made for her. She hopped into the box and gently set her mewling infant onto the soft towel. She must have been outside when her labour began, with no one home to let her in, so she'd chosen the best place she could for the birth. Now that I was home, she could bring them all inside where it was safe.

"Let's go get the others," I said, moving toward the door. But instead of following me, Cinders just looked at me then wearily sank down next to her infant, shifting and curling her body around it as it began to nuzzle against her flank.

Cinders looked up at me expectantly. My heart fell. She wanted the rest of her babies. And they needed her. But she was exhausted. The message was clear: it was up to me to get them out for her. I walked back outside to the bug-besieged bush, got down on my hands and knees, and peered into the scrubby undergrowth. The remaining babies mewled piteously, bobbing blindly for their warm mother. Above them, the worms dangled and crawled in and out amongst themselves. I swallowed, closed my eyes, and sank down onto my belly. I made myself as flat as possible and wriggled in beneath the bush until I could grasp the tiny bodies. One after the other, I pulled them all out, shuddering at the nearness of the seething mass inches from my head. Only when it was all over, did I give in to my panic. I danced around, shrieking wildly, shaking my clothing and hair, certain that I was covered with crawling caterpillars.

Once the shuddering revulsion subsided, I gathered the kittens carefully into my arms, took them inside, and placed them against their mother's warm flank. She looked up at me calmly, her purr resonating in the small room. One by one, she nosed the rest of her little family, licking them roughly and pushing them closer to her side. As she settled, she once again looked up at me—not with gratitude but as if I'd simply done what she expected I would do. It dawned on me slowly that for once, I hadn't shrunk back from an appalling task.

In that moment, Cinders gave me a rare gift. She showed me that I could be more than an insecure, bookish child, beset by fears both real and imagined. I could, if necessary, be the heroine in a story of my own making.

2

The Talented
Mr. Morris

*"Cats are a tonic, they are a laugh, they are a cuddle,
they are at least pretty just about all of the time and
beautiful some of the time."* —ROGER CARAS

ON A LOVELY SPRING AFTERNOON in 1997, four-year-old
Alexandria Tiffinger was enjoying the sunshine on the front
step with her mother, Joyce. The little girl was helping her
mother clean and polish the winter grime off her shoes when
they heard rustling sounds in the corner of their yard. A small
face peered out at them from the leaves and underbrush behind
the garden bench. "Mommy!" said the little girl. "A kitty!"

For most of her life, Joyce Tiffinger had always had at
least one cat. A portrait of Garfield, a grey longhair, with
baby Alexandria, hung in their living room. An avowed
child-hater, Garfield had been inexplicably devoted to
Alexandria; when he died, he left a void that could not easily be filled. After Garfield's death, Joyce and her husband

Dale focussed their energy on their growing daughter and their two West Highland white terriers, as well as any hungry transient felines that might come their way. "My dad kept an automatic feeder in the backyard," says Alexandria. They knew that when the time was right, they would once more share their lives with a cat.

As a long-time animal lover, Joyce was thoroughly familiar with all the neighbourhood cats. But she had never before seen the one now meandering toward them, a beautiful deep red tabby with striking mahogany markings. She went inside to find some treats and a brush, and then she and Alexandria set to pampering their unexpected guest, their shoe-cleaning forgotten. Joyce watched with delight as Alexandria fussed over him; she'd obviously inherited her parents' love for animals. But Joyce worried about her daughter's disappointment when it came time for the cat to return to wherever he'd come from. Which led to the next worry: where had he come from? And why was he out on his own? Surely someone, somewhere, was concerned about the whereabouts of this beautiful, affectionate creature? The cat had no such anxieties, however; he rubbed against Alexandria, luxuriating in her caresses, a deep rumbling purr vibrating through his body.

Then they noticed a tattoo inside his ear. Thank goodness! Now they'd be able to track down the owner and they could help get this cat safely back to where he belonged. Between veterinary hospitals and shelters, they eventually found the name and number of the person corresponding to the tattoo in the cat's ear. As Dale punched the keys on his phone, he tried not to watch Alexandria and the cat cuddling together.

"Good news!" he told the man who answered. "We've found your cat!"

"Oh." The man's one-word reply was a bit disconcerting to Dale.

After a pause, the man explained that, since he thought his cat was gone for good, he'd already replaced him. He hadn't really planned on having two cats. Although dismayed at his indifference, Dale convinced the man to come collect the wanderer, and arrangements were made to meet. Then Dale and Joyce gently reminded Alexandria that they weren't keeping the beautiful cat. He already had a home and, although they'd grown fond of him, he didn't belong to them.

On the day of the meeting, Alexandria sat outside with the cat and tearfully said her goodbyes. But the agreed-upon time came and went with no sign of the man. They phoned him again. This time he promised to be there the following day. All day they waited and once more, the man neither arrived nor contacted them to make alternate plans. Frustrated, they called him a third time and this time, he swore he'd pick up his cat over the weekend. Because the family had plans that meant they would be gone much of the weekend, Joyce gave him permission to enter their yard and retrieve his pet.

When they returned home that Sunday evening, the cat was nowhere to be found. Joyce breathed a sigh of relief that he'd finally made it back where he belonged. Alexandria, on the other hand, searched the yard eagerly, her little face drooping with disappointment when she could find no sign of her new friend. He was gone, and that was that.

Three days later, Alexandria and her mother were once more outside enjoying the spring sunshine. "The quiet of the day was suddenly broken by a soft 'meow' coming from behind the bench," remembers Alexandria. Peeking around the corner of the yard was the same pink, freckled nose and gorgeous tabby face. It was just like the first time. The little girl's heart leaped in the hope that her favourite stray had returned. "I jumped up to hug and cuddle him when I noticed something was terribly wrong," says Alexandria. She ran back, crying for her parents and yelling, "The kitty's hurt!"

Joyce and Dale rushed to see what had upset their daughter, but they weren't prepared for the scene that met them. Slowly, the ginger tabby limped through the shrubbery, exhausted and in pain. His graceful feline lope was gone; now his movements were awkward and laboured. As he pulled himself toward them, Joyce and Dale saw with horror that one back leg was hanging useless, scuffing over the grass as he walked. "Quickly, gently, my dad picked up the cat, while my mom called the emergency veterinary hospital and I sobbed in the background," says Alexandria. "Is he going to be okay?" the little girl whispered over and over. No one could answer her.

Furious, Joyce tried to imagine how the cat had ended up in their yard a second time. Had he got home, only to wander back to them? Had his owner even bothered to come to get him? They'd assumed the cat had been picked up as planned, but how could they be sure? After all, the owner had left them hanging before. Perhaps the cat had spent a lonely weekend, abandoned by his new friends, and had gone looking for company elsewhere. Then, an even worse possibility struck her: perhaps the previous owner, tired of being reminded of his obligations, had picked up his cat, driven a few kilometres away, and dumped his former pet, hoping to finally be free of him.

They would never know the circumstances around his second arrival and ultimately, it didn't matter. He was there now, back at the last place he'd found kindness.

They rushed him to the emergency veterinary hospital, where animal doctors confirmed their suspicions: the cat had most likely been hit by a car. They couldn't say how old his injuries were; they could have been inflicted anytime over the past couple of days. Joyce and Dale were horrified to think that this cat might have spent the weekend hiding his broken body, waiting in pain for them to return.

The cat was lucky to be alive, and luckier still to be getting the medical care he needed. He was badly dehydrated and suffering from shock, but worst of all, he had sustained a severe hind leg fracture. "His leg was shattered," Alexandria explains, "broken in seven places and impossible to save." They were told there were only two options for the cat: euthanasia or amputation. Given that his owner had abandoned him, and that he now required extensive—not to

mention expensive—surgery to recover from his injury, euthanasia was a reasonable decision. But should this animal
have to pay the price of a thoughtless, irresponsible man's
actions? When Joyce and Dale looked at the stricken face of
their little girl, they knew that whatever the cost, they would
be bringing a three-legged cat home with them.

It took a full week of fluids and nursing care before Mr.
Morris, as they'd begun calling him, was stable enough for
surgery. Because of his fragile condition, he needed overnight care as well, so every evening the Tiffinger family
transferred him from their regular veterinarian to the after-
hours emergency hospital. Every morning, they picked him
up and took him back. After the surgery, it took yet another
week for him to recover from the amputation sufficiently to
be released. "Mr. Morris was finally ready to go to his new
home," says Alexandria. "My home." There was no question
about it now. After everything they'd gone through together,
he belonged to them.

It would take him considerable time to adjust to his new
life on three legs. "With an elastic sock on his other hind leg
and the rear half of his body, and many stitches, he slowly
learned to hop," says Alexandria. "But it took him at least a
couple of months to completely figure it out."

Slowly, his lush mahogany coat grew back to cover the
jagged scar. His muscles returned to their full, rippling
glory and he regained the weight he'd lost. By Christmas,
Mr. Morris was perfectly healthy. He'd learned to use his

remaining limbs to compensate for the missing one, and sometimes it was easy to forget that he'd lost one at all. "He could run incredibly fast and had a surprising amount of energy," recalls Alexandria.

But the most astonishing thing about him was his love for people. Throughout his ordeal, the pain, the fear, and the loneliness, never once did he show any sign of irritation for his caregivers. "He purred—and still does to this day—for everyone that walked in the door," she says with a smile. Being discarded and forgotten by his first owner hadn't dented his friendliness; even the pain he'd endured throughout his injury hadn't shaken his trustful nature.

Then, about halfway through January, Mr. Morris began to look a bit peaked. He didn't seem to want to play as much and he began to pick at his meals. It soon became obvious that something was drastically wrong. He wouldn't eat or drink; all he wanted to do was sleep. Back they went to the animal hospital, where x-rays revealed a round object lodged in his intestine. "They had no idea what it was, but it clearly had to be removed," says Alexandria. Once more, Mr. Morris went under the surgeon's knife and once more the family huddled together, hoping that he'd come back to them whole and healthy. "When we picked up Mr. Morris, the tech handed us a medicine vial with 'Mr. Morris' written on the front. Inside was a dime that they had found inside him." How it had got inside him and how long it had been there remains a mystery.

Several years passed relatively uneventfully, a relief for

the Tiffinger family. Mr. Morris remained healthy and happy and welcomed the addition of a lovely tortoiseshell named Flora. One weekend, Alexandria visited a local cat show for the first time. She walked up and down the aisles of cat cages, admiring the many different breeds and colours and talking with the owners. Then she watched a couple of classes compete. The judge first lined up the entries, looked them over as a group and then handled each animal individually before assigning the ribbons. The cats sat calmly throughout the event; some even preened and posed especially for the judge! Apparently showmanship played just as big a role as beauty.

Alexandria noticed with surprise that not all the cats were a particular breed; some looked like ordinary house cats. She was right. In addition to the purebred divisions, which showcase the Siamese, Persians, Burmese, Himalayans, and various other pedigreed felines, cat fancier clubs allow non-pedigreed cats to compete in the Household Pet class. This opens the show world to people who aren't interested in breeding their cats, but want to enjoy the fun of exhibiting their special pets.

Seven-year-old Alexandria thought it would be fun to enter. Between Flora's beauty and Mr. Morris's charm, she just knew they'd be bringing home ribbons. She entered them in the next show in the Household Pet division and before she knew it, she was hooked. Alexandria quickly discovered that, while Flora didn't enjoy the hustle and bustle of the show ring, Mr. Morris shone in the spotlight. Before long, he'd received

Mr. Morris

the title of Supreme Grand Champion Household Pet Cat, as well as regional awards from the International Cat Association. Mr. Morris was a star! And Alexandria and her parents made a whole crowd of new friends.

"The people are incredible," she says. "I'm the youngest member of the club." Showing a cat is a lot of hard work, but Alexandria had help learning the ropes. A few days before the show, each cat must be bathed, a learning experience in itself, dried, and brushed. Immediately before entering the ring, they are brushed again. Then they wait to be called to the benching area, where the judges assess the class as a group. "When your number's called, you groom your cat, comb the fur around his face to enlarge his mane, and put him in his cage," she explains. "With Mr. Morris, he was usually the only red tabby so he usually won Best of Colour. If there were other tabbies, he might get first or second or third or whatever in that division. It's not like the purebreds, where you can win Best of Breed."

Mr. Morris began to develop a following. "Lots of the long-time exhibitors and spectators remember Mr. Morris!" says Alexandria. "They ask about him, and cheer for him if he's competing." He's had his photo in newspapers and magazines, alongside interviews with Alexandria and other club members. "The *Edmonton Journal* once had an article about the 10 best things to do over the weekend," adds Alexandria, "and they mentioned the cat show and included his picture."

It wasn't long before a third cat, a skittish character they named Sequoia, joined Mr. Morris and Flora. "Sequoia would not come near anybody when we first got him," says Alexandria. "He was very scared. But he's three now and he's realized that he's part of our family."

Then one day, during one of Mr. Morris's routine examinations, the veterinarian suggested to Alexandria that, because of his remarkable disposition, her cat might be a good candidate for pet therapy. She loved the idea immediately, but when she contacted the Pet Therapy Society of Northern Alberta, she found out that they'd never had a cat in their program before; all their temperament tests were geared toward dogs.

They were also reluctant to admit such a young child into the program. "I was only 10," says Alexandria. "You have to be 16 to do it alone, because there are criminal checks and everything." Finally, they agreed to allow Alexandria and Mr. Morris to participate in the initial testing, provided Joyce accompanied them.

They had to take Mr. Morris for a screening test before being allowed into the seminar. The test was held in the back of a dog-grooming studio, filled with all sorts of strange smells and sounds. Agility obstacles and pylons were placed on the ground; metal objects crashed and banged, and strangers walked by with brooms. "He had to sit for 30 seconds without moving," says Alexandria. She placed him in the middle of the melee and he sat down calmly, interested in this strange place but not at all alarmed. After being handled by judges and gawked at by crowds of spectators, this, he seemed to say, was a cakewalk. He passed the first hurdle and began training with a group of seven dogs.

The instructors explained to the group the other requirements of therapy pets and their handlers. In addition to tolerating loud noises and unfamiliar smells, the animals—Mr. Morris included—had to walk calmly on a leash. He had to be able to pass by another animal without becoming distracted. He also had to be able to withstand the temptation of unguarded food. Hospital patients often have snacks nearby and a therapy pet must never take food unless it's offered. Not only is it rude, but it could be dangerous to the animal if the food contained medication.

On June 22, 2003, Alexandria and Mr. Morris graduated

from the pet therapy program. "Mr. Morris passed all the courses with flying colours," says Alexandria proudly. The next step was for the new therapy pets to begin doing practicum visits alongside experienced handlers. They went to Good Samaritan, a nursing home for disabled adults, where they quickly became favourite visitors. "One of the patients, Michelle, had been in a wheelchair since childhood," says Alexandria, "but she'd had cats and was quite interested in Mr. Morris." Another patient, a woman named Linda with multiple sclerosis, also grew to love Mr. Morris's weekly visits. And Mr. Morris got to know them, too. "We used a fleecy pad, because he sheds so much," says Alexandria. "He'd sit on the chair beside them and let them groom him. Mr. Morris loves to be groomed. He starts purring like crazy."

As with their experience in the show ring, the pair became very popular, but it turned out that Mr. Morris and Alexandria had a bigger task ahead of them. When Alexandria was 11 years old, Joyce became ill and could no longer accompany her daughter. Because Dale had not done the training, he couldn't pinch-hit for his wife; Alexandria and Mr. Morris were forced to leave the program. His formal role as a therapy pet had come to an end, but his task of giving comfort was about to become much more difficult.

Alexandria missed her work at the hospital, but she had bigger things to worry about: doctors had discovered a malignant mass on one of Joyce's lungs.

Just when she thought things couldn't get worse, her father

also got sick. "Mom got lung cancer," says Alexandria, "and then Dad got thyroid cancer." In the next few months, Dale had two operations to remove first one side, then the other, of the affected thyroid gland, and Joyce was scheduled for major thoracic surgery. Right around the time Joyce was in hospital having a large portion of lung removed, Dale was undergoing radiation therapy, the second part of his treatment, to destroy any tumour cells that might have eluded the surgeons.

It was a very challenging time for the Tiffinger family and fate wasn't done with them yet. Joyce was in post-operative recovery and had barely regained consciousness when she began hemorrhaging from a ruptured pulmonary artery. Within minutes, she was back on the operating table, where surgeons worked frantically to repair the damage. They were successful, but it was a close call. "She lost a rib and was in a lot of pain," remembers Alexandria. "She spent eight days in the hospital."

Few things are more frightening for children than seeing their parents sick and in pain. Each day, Dale, who was still dealing with the after-effects of surgery and radiation, drove to his daughter's school, picked her up, and headed for the hospital. Sometimes they picked up burgers or sandwiches on the way. For the rest of the day, Alexandria curled up in a chair at her mother's bedside. When Joyce was strong enough, Alexandria perched at the edge of the bed and they held hands and talked. It never took long, however, for Joyce's strength to fade. Then she'd simply drift in and out on a tide of narcotics while Alexandria did her grade-five homework.

Alexandria was grateful that they could be together, but it was excruciating to have to keep her distance. "I couldn't hug Mom because she was in too much pain," says Alexandria. "I couldn't even touch Dad because he was shedding radiation." Radiation is an efficient weapon against cancer cells, but it is this very aspect that makes it dangerous. Until it had cleared his system, Dale had to follow strict isolation protocol to prevent his household from becoming contaminated. "Everything he touched had to be disposable," says Alexandria.

But she had no choice; she had to be content with being able to see them, and talk to them, and be in the same room. Sometimes, after her homework was done, she could crawl onto the bed beside Joyce. Dale would pull up a chair beside them and the three of them watched TV together. It was a façade of normalcy, but they all clung to it. After a few hours, Alexandria gently kissed her mother goodbye and went home with her father for the night.

The house seemed big and dark and empty that spring. Alexandria had no siblings to share her fears, so relied on her many friends—and her cats. Flora, Sequoia, and Mr. Morris anxiously followed them around, eager for their company after each long, quiet day. Dale couldn't pet the cats, so it fell to Alexandria to reassure them that they were still loved and cared for. This she did gladly, and each stroke earned rough purrs and warm head-butts; the cats poured themselves into the cold, empty, hurting space just above her stomach. Each night, she crawled into bed, pulled a warm furry body into her arms and allowed herself to cry.

Before they'd gone into hospital, Joyce and Dale knew that their daughter would need to find something to take her mind off the fear she'd been living with for the past few months. Over the years, they'd watched their enterprising child win ribbons with Mr. Morris and make friends among the other competitors; perhaps the time was right for her to move out of the Household Pet division and into the more challenging world of purebreds. The perfect solution arrived in the form of a tiny rust-coloured curly-haired kitten, a registered purebred Cornish Rex named Little Red Baron. "Baron came at Easter that year," remembers Alexandria. "It was nice to have a little kitten at that time."

That spring, the family simply focussed on getting through as best they could. Being surrounded by cats helped the entire family recover from their difficult winter, and Baron, like all kittens, was a source of endless amusement. All the cats gloried in the abundance of human companionship suddenly returned to them. "Once Mom came home, there was always one cat with each of us," says Alexandria, "because there were four of them and only three of us!"

Little Red Baron quickly developed a close bond with Sequoia, and the two were seldom separated. "Sequoia and Baron are the mischief-makers," says Alexandria. "Sequoia, who has extra toes on his paws, opens the cupboard doors. Then Baron hops in and gets a bag of food and they both eat."

Alexandria was excited about showing her new prospect. Gorgeous, graceful Baron has the same mahogany markings as Mr. Morris, and she had high hopes for him in the show ring. Baron, unfortunately, wasn't comfortable with the idea initially. They brought Sequoia along for company, but that didn't help. He apparently agreed with Baron's opinion of the whole event. So Alexandria decided to bring Mr. Morris—the old pro—along as support for Baron. Under Mr. Morris's calming influence, Baron relaxed and allowed his model persona to shine.

Now a seasoned veteran, Baron has also made many friends among the other feline competitors and doesn't need to have Mr. Morris at his side. But sometimes, Mr. Morris is there, anyway, just to greet his fans.

And Mr. Morris continues his hospital work occasionally, too. "I still take him, periodically, to short therapy sessions with the Edmonton Cat Fanciers Club, usually a couple times a year," says Alexandria.

No one knows what the future holds for Alexandria and Mr. Morris, but their history has prepared them well for the struggles ahead. "Although he is now 12 years old— the same age as I am—and retired from both showbiz and therapy work, Mr. Morris continues to be a great therapist for all three of us at home," says Alexandria.

3

The Sweet, Sweet Smell of Home

"Cats are a mysterious kind of folk. There is more passing in their minds than we are aware of."
—SIR WALTER SCOTT

THE TINY KITTEN SAT IN a cage at the Ottawa Humane Society, blinking in sleepy confusion at the strange sights and sounds around him. Edith Donnelly should have known better. The approaching Christmas season accentuated the sense of loss that hovered over her, now that her cat family had shrunk from two to one. She knew she was vulnerable, that she shouldn't make any rash decisions, but she wanted another cat. Was it too soon? She stuck her finger between the bars again and the little mite pawed at them playfully. He was scrawny with gingery patches on white fur and a feathery ginger-coloured tail. But it was his beautiful green eyes that caught her attention: they were two very different sizes. As she looked at him, she knew it was too late for rational thought.

"His funny little mismatched eyes begged me to take him home with me," says Edith, "but I decided that a big cat and an enormous dog created enough vacuuming for one person. Besides, I couldn't always be rescuing the lonely, the hungry, and the pitiful. I felt guilty, but I did manage to walk away."

However, she mentioned the kitten to her sister Janet. Janet, who knew that Edith wouldn't have said anything if she weren't already smitten, secretly made arrangements to have the kitten presented to her as an early Christmas gift. Shocked and overjoyed, Edith named him Bentley, after the car of her dreams.

Bentley settled in quickly, oblivious to the usual house rules. Edith's collie Bailey and her elderly Persian cat Doo-dah looked askance at this tornado that had been dropped on their quiet existence. Bentley leaped onto the kitchen counters; he stuck his little nose into everyone else's food dishes; he jumped with all four feet into a baking dish full of milk while Edith was preparing rice pudding. "And after he used the litter box," says Edith, "every window in the house had to be opened full tilt!" Only when he slept were they able to relax, and even then, he had the nerve to settle into Edith's bed as if he owned it, curling up and snoring like an old man. Bailey and Doo-dah shot evil glances at the upstart who'd taken such liberties, but he didn't even notice.

Three days later, Edith noticed that the smaller of his eyes had suddenly closed up completely. A trip to the veterinary hospital revealed that what she'd originally thought was an enchanting anomaly was actually a dangerous congenital birth defect. The eye had developed a nasty infection and Ben had quickly become a very sick kitten. "One eye was swollen, just a terrible mess," says Edith. "But a minor surgical procedure and several prescriptions later, I found myself writing a check for $680. I drove home wondering what in the world I had done to myself, and better yet, why?"

When they returned home from the animal hospital, she had her answer. As soon as she opened the door of the carry-cage, Ben shot out and darted directly to the La-Z-Boy chair by the sunny front window where Doo-dah spent most of his time. Edith braced herself for fireworks, but they never came. "Watching this little white fluffball jump into the chair and curl up in the scoop of Doo-dah's body was totally surprising, but so very endearing," recalls Edith. "Ben, at that special moment, was truly adopted." Ben's illness had brought out a nurturing aspect to Doo-dah's personality. The old cat had apparently decided that this little one needed someone to look out for him, keep him warm, bathe him, and teach him what he needed to know. "He essentially became a surrogate mom even though he was very much a male cat," says Edith. At 14 years of age, Doo-dah's energy level, his grooming pattern, and his playfulness were all renewed. Bentley, it seems, came as much for Doo-dah as he did for Edith.

That same winter, Edith became very ill herself, suffering a collapsed lung. Unable to work, she seldom went out during that time, and she and Ben spent long weeks together resting and recuperating. By the time spring rolled around, they'd both regained their health, and the bond they shared was unbreakable. "He was my baby," she says.

Although Doo-dah had learned to love little Ben, his elderly body simply couldn't keep up with the demands of a playful kitten. "I worked at an assembly factory at the time and took Ben to work with me, to give Doo-dah some quiet time," says Edith. "He'd hang around me or get into mischief. He liked to climb onto the tallest box on the shelf and not come down, especially at quitting time." Edith loved Ben's company during the day, and her co-workers enjoyed the entertainment he brought to the workplace.

From then on, things settled into the normal ebb and flow of cat–human relationships. "I was allowed to continue to live in the house as long as I obeyed all the rules by providing many back-scratches, timely meals, fresh litter boxes, and new squeaky toys," says Edith.

Although Ben was raised to be an indoor cat, he managed to escape from time to time. "He was a Houdini cat," emphasizes Edith. "I could keep him in, but if someone else came to the door, it was the perfect opportunity to escape and he took it." A sardine dangled around his usual haunts was enough to flush him out, and Edith could usually get him back inside in short order.

But one day, he was nowhere to be found. "I'd no idea that he'd escaped at first," she says. "He'd been gone for at least an hour when he didn't show up for dinner and I realized he'd got out." She wasn't worried at the start; after all, Ben had got out before. He'd never stayed out all night, so Edith expected him back before dark. She walked around outside, shaking bags of treats and calling his name. She enlisted her neighbours in the search. She turned the microwave timer on, in the hope that this favourite dinnertime sound would do the trick. No response.

When bedtime arrived and he still wasn't back, she felt the first pangs of fear. She told herself to calm down and be reasonable. After all, the weather was beautiful, warm, and dry. He wasn't in any real danger. "It was so nice outside, I thought he might have crawled under the house and gone to sleep," she adds. "I finally went to bed, but left all the lights on outside the house and the breezeway doors wide open, fully believing he'd be back during the night."

But he wasn't. Now it was time for action. With her sister Janet's help, Edith printed "Lost" posters and hung them on every available mailbox and street lamp. They went to the humane society to see if he had been caught and taken to the shelter, but none of the cages held their familiar odd-eyed Bentley. Day after day, Edith called, asking about him, but the answer was the same. No one had reported a sighting of a cat matching Bentley's description. Then she heard the worst possible news: two blocks away, a car had just struck a cat matching Ben's description. His body was still lying on the side of the road. "I had to go look, but I couldn't bear to get out of the car and look closely," says Edith. While the markings on this poor cat were similar, Edith could see from a distance that it wasn't Ben. Relief swept over her, only to be replaced once more by fear. Ben was still missing.

The next day as Edith was receiving a delivery, she mentioned Ben's disappearance to the courier, who suggested she hang something outside, as high as possible, with a scent that the cat would recognize. "Oh lucky day!" says Edith wryly. "Doo-dah had thrown up on my comforter that very morning." She scrambled to get it out of the laundry basket, hoping that Doo-dah's dreaded hairball combined with her own scent would be strong enough to pull Ben back to the two companions that loved him most in the world. Then she pinned it to the clothesline, pulled the line taut, and crossed her fingers.

"On the sixth day, there was a logbook notation [at the humane society] of someone seeing a white and orange cat in a tree," says Edith. "It had been there four or five days." Chances were slim that this was her cat. The tree was in the downtown area, south of Parliament Hill, about a 10-minute drive from Edith's house. How could Ben have even got to that part of town? Also, he was declawed; he wasn't likely able to climb a tree. The report added that when attempts were made to climb up and rescue the cat, it clambered to a higher branch. Still, Edith couldn't help but hope it was Ben, in spite of the factors that didn't fit. "It sounded possible," she remembers. "The colours were right. The timing was right. But the report came from downtown and I lived in the west end of the city—not entirely impossible, but I wasn't going to count on this being good news."

A long shot was better than no leads at all, so Edith and Janet drove to the address on the report, fully armed with his carry-cage, pictures of Ben and Doo-dah cuddled up together, and, of course, sardines. They first went to talk with the person who had originally called the humane society, but were told that the cat had been gone when she'd looked out that morning. The woman speculated he'd probably fallen out of the tree. Edith and Janet couldn't argue; after all, with nothing to eat or drink for almost a week, Ben's strength must be fading. "We walked the neighbourhood, house to house, showing the pictures, and hoping against hope," Edith says. "We called his name over and over and over. We crawled under fences, through garbage sheds, and peered under cars. Finally, we gave up and headed home. There were no words spoken in the car all the way back."

Janet went back across the street to her own home, and Edith went about her usual chores, trying to push away the grief that had begun welling up inside her. Doo-dah and Bailey still needed her attention, but she had to force herself to focus on them. "At about 4 o'clock I yanked on the side-pulley to raise the comforter to the highest possible position on the clothesline," says Edith. "Then I set about feeding the other two animals."

Meals completed, she let Bailey out the back door and as the latch clicked, she stood meditatively, waiting for the dog to return. The sun was beginning its descent on the horizon, cutting a warm swath through the trees and she shaded her eyes against the brightness. Then something caught her eye, a flash of movement, light-coloured against the green of the yard. "It was Ben, bounding across the backyard at the speed of a greyhound!" says Edith. "He fairly flew up onto the deck and scrambled up my back onto my shoulders. I let out one teary-eyed screech that was probably heard for blocks: 'Ben's home!'" Edith was laughing and crying and shaking all at the same time. Ben was purring, meowing, and digging his back claws into her skin, but she didn't even feel it.

"My sister had put so much effort into this, it's too bad she missed the moment," says Edith, "but, oh boy, she heard me! Everyone heard me!"

Ben was exhausted, hungry, thirsty, and disheveled, but all he wanted to do was cry and purr and reconnect with his family. Doo-dah and Bailey sniffed him over carefully, clearly glad to see him again. Finally, Ben settled down enough to have something to eat. Then, for the first time in a week, Edith turned out the lights and went to bed, secure in the knowledge that Ben was back where he belonged, with them.

The next day, Edith and Janet went about the neighbourhood, replacing the "Lost" posters with "Ben's Home!" posters, and joyfully telling anyone who would listen about his return. Friends, neighbours, co-workers, and even complete strangers shared their excitement at Ben's safe return. "People were coming to my house and welling up with tears," she recalls. "It was a very emotional time. Everyone was so happy." No one was happier than Ben, and six years later, he's still happy to remain close to home.

So how did Ben get downtown? "We believe he had innocently hopped through the open window into Janet's car—which of course was familiar to him—intending to take a snooze," says Edith. "A little later, she drove a friend home who lived only a few blocks from the address of the person who reported seeing him." When the car stopped, Ben probably jumped out only to panic when he discovered that he was on an unfamiliar street filled with heavy traffic. "He's deathly afraid of the sound of trucks and motorcycles," says Edith, "and if he'd heard anything like that, he'd have done anything in his power to get away."

Edith also believes that by walking up and down the streets of that neighbourhood, they provided a reminder of his "home-scent." The distance that took 10 minutes to drive would have turned into an hour-long sprint for Ben; he must have come out of hiding just in time to watch them drive away. But seeing Edith and Janet was enough for him to overcome his fear and make a break for safety, running the entire way. He only paused to sniff the air, testing for his lifeline, the comforter on the clothesline that would lead him back to safety. "Of course," Edith admits, "we can only speculate on this part: Ben's not talking."

CHAPTER

4

Fritz, the Community Cat

"Cats don't belong to people. They belong to places."
—WRIGHT MORRIS

ON SUN-BAKED SALT SPRING Island, on the west coast of British Columbia, midway between the main town of Ganges and the village of Vesuvius, sits an old church, now known as Central Hall. The community hall, which doubles as a cinema, is a natural meeting place for residents. Besides movie viewing, the building serves whatever purpose is needed at the time, from fitness club to voting station.

One day about 10 years ago, a longhaired white and brown cat was seen lounging outside the door of the cinema. Cathie Newman was president of the local SPCA at the time. "One of the young fellows that worked at the cinema came to tell me about this cat that was hanging around," she says. They'd been giving him scraps of food, and they really liked him, but he wasn't neutered and the tomcat odour was becoming an issue. "They asked us to take care of him," explains Cathie. So, the SPCA neutered him, cleaned him up, and sent him back to the cinema.

No one knew where he'd come from, but no one objected. Salt Spring Island prides itself on being an accepting community. Within days, it was clear that the big cat considered himself at home, spending most of his time sitting on top of the phone booth, watching the comings and goings of his townspeople. His relaxed demeanour fit perfectly with the island mentality of Salt Spring residents and before long, he'd become known across the island as Fritz, the Cinema Cat. "He's not the prettiest looking cat," says Cathie. "He looks like somebody socked him in the eye. But he's interesting and that's more important than pretty."

Sometimes, interesting cats belonging to "everyone" become neglected cats, cared for by none; that's not the case with Fritz. Michael Levy, the cinema's projectionist, became accustomed to greeting Fritz at the start of each workday and began keeping an eye on him. Michael's brother Geoff built a house for Fritz, and not just an ordinary cat shelter. This one boasts inch-thick insulation, a retractable roof, two picture windows, a sheepskin rug, and even a deck. "He's absolutely spoiled silly," says Cathie.

Although he's part of the community, Cathie brings him food each morning and, as she now works at a veterinary clinic, is able to take responsibility for his medical needs.

"He's become *my* cat," says Cathie. Recently Fritz was in for his annual checkup. "Everything was great," reports Cathie, "so I put a note in our newspaper to let everyone know that he's lost a bit of the extra weight he'd been carrying, his tests were all good, and he's got all his vaccinations. People were so happy that I put the note in the paper! They all want to keep informed about Fritz."

He makes friends constantly. "The other day someone told me, 'Oh I think Fritz has a new friend,'" says Cathie. "Sure enough, there was a young man sitting on the curb, looked like he was waiting for his ride. The two of them were just sitting there looking at each other, chatting away, like they were talking politics or something." Fritz stretches and bends along with the exercise enthusiasts during the seniors' Tai Chi class. "One time," says Cathie with a laugh, "he was grooming himself, sticking his back leg in the air, and it looked just like he was doing Tai Chi himself!"

He silently witnesses the drop of ballots on election day and joins in funeral processions at the cemetery behind the hall. On sunny days, he perches on the top of the phone booth outside the cinema, greeting moviegoers as any good host. "He just loves that," adds Cathie. "The more people the better."

But one Sunday evening in 2005, Fritz's friendliness got him into trouble. Michael Levy arrived for his shift to discover that Fritz was missing from his usual post. He looked around, thinking that the cat must have just found a different spot, but there was no sign of him.

"He's gone! He's gone!" said a frantic witness. "She took him!"

"Who?" asked Michael. Everyone on the island knew and loved Fritz. Who would do such a thing? The witness described the kidnapper as an unknown woman driving a small red car. She'd scooped Fritz up, put him into a cat carrier, and driven off with him.

Michael phoned Cathie, who phoned the next person and the one after that. Emergency measures were called for and an army of angry volunteers sprang into action. It's not unusual to see Salt Spring Island residents protesting something. The population is made up of everything from rich, blue-haired condo-dwellers to dreadlocked, tree-hugging campers; everyone is passionate and willing to defend their beliefs. "There's a lot of diverse opinions, and people get their shorts in a knot over just about everything," says Cathie. "But Fritz is one of the few things on this island that we all agree on." Throughout the night, cellphones beeped and rang across the island. People were frantic and furious. Clearly, this was no one anyone knew. Everyone on Salt Spring knew that Fritz belonged in front of the cinema, and that he was well cared for and happy in his chosen home.

Hour after hour their desperation grew. Who knew what this person might have wanted with Fritz? They hoped it was simply a well-meaning, but ill-advised act of benevolence. But everyone knew that there are those few people in the

Fritz

world who take vicious pleasure in abusing small animals. Surely Fritz wouldn't end up at the mercy of such a person!

The furor reached beyond the hearts of private residents into the public arena. The RCMP immediately sent two squad cars to investigate the crime scene. Local SPCA officials marshalled their forces. The chamber of commerce contacted a network of local businesses, asking them to be on the lookout for this outsider who'd so blatantly stolen their Salt Spring icon.

The beauty of living on an island is that there's only one way off: the ferry. This thief would be caught. The little group rolled up their sleeves, ready to rescue Fritz and repay any harm that might have befallen him. At each of the three ferry terminals on the island, workers went on high alert. Police officers threatened to lay charges of theft if they caught her. Volunteers fanned out, looking for a red subcompact with a cat carrier inside. "The entire island was in an uproar," recalls Cathie. "We all stationed ourselves at the ferry terminals. We weren't going to let her get off the island with him."

Then the next morning, another phone call: Fritz was back! No one witnessed the event, but suddenly there was Fritz, once more lounging happily in his cathouse, as if nothing had ever happened. The abductor had apparently got wind of the overwhelming response of the island residents. The quiet, surreptitious rescue operation she'd planned had blown up into a catastrophe of unseen proportions. Her intentions, it appears, were pure. She wanted to improve Fritz's life but she wasn't planning on bloodshed or jail time! So, under the cover of darkness, she returned Fritz to the front of the cinema and made her escape. "The woman heard about the posse waiting for her," says Cathie.

It turned out the "criminal" was a long-time cat rescuer from the Vancouver area who believed the traffic at the intersection in front of the cinema posed a threat to Fritz's life. She was under the impression that Fritz was a homeless, ownerless cat who would have a better life if he were placed in a more "stable" environment. "We were all so surprised to hear she thought he was in such danger," says Cathie in amazement. " I mean, he's almost nine years old now. If he was in such danger, how had he survived for so long?"

The woman made one simple mistake: she assumed that a cat without a family is ownerless and that a cat without an address is homeless. Most of the time, for most cats, this is true. But not for Fritz, the Cinema Cat.

Fritz is now back to his laid-back lifestyle of meeting and greeting his old friends, overseeing their fitness projects, watching movies with them, and generally enjoying the quiet ebb and flow of island life. The residents of Salt Spring Island value Fritz more than ever now, taking pride in their unusual mascot and their ability to pull together to defend one of their own. They proved that not every "home" looks the same and that the bond they have with Fritz makes them all family, despite their differences. Fritz is most definitely a community cat, with home and family across the entire island.

In February 2007, Fritz was hit by a car outside Central Hall and killed. There were numerous tributes to him in the local paper and a memorial service was held in the hall. Louise Adela Nye has written and self-published two books about Fritz: Fritz the Cinema Cat *and* Fritz Gets His Wings.

5

Against
the Odds

*"Our perfect companions never have fewer
than four feet."* —COLETTE

ONE COOL MISTY MORNING, ON rough road lined with the immense ancient trees of the Stave Lake wilderness area north of Mission, British Columbia, a small shape caught the eye of a forest ranger as he drove to work. He slowed the vehicle to a stop, got out and scanned the thick undergrowth. Then he saw it: a cat, a very skinny young calico cat. There were no houses around for kilometres. Where had this cat come from?

He squatted down and beckoned. The cat scrambled toward him, rubbing her face against his hands and mewing. She looked at him with such desperation, such need, that the ranger knew he couldn't leave her. But how could he help? He scooped her into his arms and set her on the seat beside him. Then he drove back into Mission and headed for the Fraser

Valley Humane Society. They would know what to do.

The Fraser Valley Humane Society was founded in 1999 by a group of people concerned about the lack of care for animals, cats in particular, in the Mission area. Executive Director Charlene MacDonald says that while the surrounding cities all had SPCA shelters, the District of Mission had only a city pound, and it refused to take cats.

Mission's sprawling hillside neighbourhoods interspersed with farmland make it a popular dumping ground for unwanted cats. "There's one area of Mission where 90 percent of the cats are there because they've been dumped," says Charlene. "It's awful. You can sit in your car after dark and just watch them run back and forth across the road." To survive, they learn to steal food, fight for territory, and hide from people. Although they might once have been cherished family pets, they are destined to become unhealthy, slinking creatures of the night and any kittens they hide in nooks and crannies are feral.

This is the situation the volunteers and board members of the Fraser Valley Humane Society are determined to mend. Colonies of feral cats are trapped, spayed or neutered, vaccinated, and re-released to the humans who care for them from a distance. Stray cats are taken into care and every attempt is made to reunite them with their families. All kittens are spayed or neutered before being placed in homes. It's Charlene's goal to see every cat in a home, and no unwanted kittens born, ever. "We will do it," she emphasizes.

It's a lofty goal, but they can only attack the problem one cat at a time. Some of the stories are heart-breaking. Brant, a handsome orange male who came to the shelter after being hit by a car. Angel, a gentle, sweet-natured girl who was found in a ditch and gave birth the next day. Brigeit, thrown off the bridge from a car window. Maria, found abandoned in a box.

The day the forest ranger came to the shelter with the thin calico cat, she was logged into the admission book, given food and water and a clean place to sleep. According to Danielle Allen, vice-president of the FVHS board of directors, the cat was in rough shape. "He said it must have been abandoned because he found it five kilometres up a logging road in a deeply forested area," says Danielle. "He said it must have been awfully hungry because it eagerly came right to him."

Upon entering the shelter, each cat is given a name; this one became Spirit. They put her under 24-hour observation until a veterinary appointment could be made, but the next morning they noticed that something was wrong with Spirit. She was anxious and uncomfortable. Then she rolled over on her side, revealing a row of swollen, engorged nipples on her abdomen. Danielle and the volunteers faced a horrifying reality: Spirit had just given birth, probably within the last few days. Somewhere, out there in the wilderness, a litter of newborn kittens waited, cold, damp, and hungry, for their mother to return.

"Never believing tiny kittens could have survived the

night, I tried to forget about yet another animal tragedy," says Danielle. They focussed on caring for Spirit and preparing her to be spayed, vaccinated, and moved to a permanent home. But Spirit could not forget. All day she paced in her cage, the exhaustion of the previous day gone. "It was almost as if the previous day of food, water, and rest had rejuvenated her," says Danielle. But as the day wore on it was apparent that Spirit was becoming frantic. Danielle talked to Charlene about going up into the area where Spirit was found, to have a look for the kittens. Charlene agreed that it was worth a try. She recruited her kitten-loving dog and they were on their way. "'Heavily forested' did not even begin to describe the side of the mountain where we mounted our search," says Danielle. "After 20 minutes we both realized there were thousands of hiding places and we would need more help if we were to ever find Spirit's kittens."

Danielle returned to the shelter with a heavy heart, knowing that nothing would soothe Spirit but to find her babies. "It was tough the next day, knowing I would have to look at Spirit and tell her we did the best we could," she says. But then Danielle realized that they'd forgotten that there was one creature that knew exactly where the kittens were hidden. Spirit herself could lead them to her babies. But would she do it? "One look into her pleading eyes and I knew what I had to do," says Danielle.

They outfitted Spirit with a harness and leash to be sure they'd be able to follow her without losing her again. Cats rarely take such restraints willingly, but Spirit appeared to understand the urgency and acquiesced without a murmur. Once more Danielle headed up into the bush, but this time Spirit was in charge. "And after searching just over an hour, Spirit led me to her three ice-cold, one-week old kittens," says Danielle. "They'd been hidden under a tree stump by a very careful mother over 55 hours earlier."

The entire shelter cheered to see this tiny feline family reunited. It took several hours in an incubator for the kittens, two girls and one boy, to recover from their ordeal. By the next day, however, both mom and babies had settled in, and were given a clean bill of health. Later, the veterinarian who examined the kittens admitted that they were only minutes away from death when they were found.

For animal rescue workers, nothing is more satisfying than a happy ending; knowing that Spirit and her babies are in permanent loving homes is the best possible outcome. Sometimes, however, circumstances don't allow cats to be placed immediately. Whenever the shelter staff have a long-term cat to care for, it's inevitable that they become especially bonded to it, and in the spring of 2005, another cat was found wandering in Mission, one that was destined to become a favourite.

At first glance, when the grey-and-white tabby was admitted to the shelter, he looked like the many other thin, unkempt, homeless cats they dealt with day after day. But, as the good Samaritan who found him pointed out with distress, something was definitely wrong with this cat. He appeared to have a "hole" in his neck. Arrangements were made to have him examined by a veterinarian.

The veterinarian reassured them that the injury on his neck looked like an abscess, a common enough occurrence, especially in outdoor cats. But once the cat was sedated and they could probe more deeply, they discovered other, far more extensive injuries. The abscess was the least of his worries; beneath the fur on the bridge of his nose, the cat had a large, healed-over scar and inside his mouth, he had several broken teeth. What had happened to this cat?

They carried him into the x-ray room. Perhaps radiographs could explain his strange injuries. The films were processed and clipped up to the viewer. Bright light shone eerily against the skeletal feline image, white areas of bone contrasting with the black and grey of less dense material. Inside the skull, in addition to the many tiny bones and teeth that form the complex structures of a cat's head, a scattering of white shards glowed brightly. They had their answer: this cat had been shot in the face.

The pellets had not penetrated his skull into his brain, which is why he survived, nor had they caused obvious damage to his eyes. But the metal had literally exploded on impact, embedding bits of shrapnel into the bone and soft tissue of his mouth and neck. As the wounds healed over, the fragments began to migrate through the layers of flesh, searching for bone in which to rest.

They had their answer, but it gave rise to another question. What could they do about it? Removing the shrapnel would require horribly invasive surgery; even with surgery, it would be impossible to find every little sliver of metal. Dodge, as they'd come to call him, didn't appear to be in pain, despite his wounds, and he'd perked up tremendously with some nourishment and rest. Then there was the issue of money, an ever-present worry for the shelter. There was no owner to consent to treatment or take financial responsibility for it.

Charlene decided to wait, in the hope that an owner could be located. The shelter began an exhaustive search. But since Dodge had no collar or tattoo, they didn't have much to go on. In the meantime, the cat was neutered, tattooed, vaccinated, and treated for fleas and worms, so he'd one day be eligible for adoption.

"I first met Dodge shortly after I had begun volunteering at the humane society cleaning the new isolation unit," says Cathy Hamm, who now volunteers on the board of directors for the society. To keep him from licking his wound, he'd been fitted with an Elizabethan collar, a necessary but awkward device that turned him into a walking disaster area. "He was very thin and dirty and because of the cone, he'd overturned everything in his crate making a frightening mess. His face was torn up and he had stitches everywhere. I was reluctant to even touch him but he was scheduled for medications and I had to clean his crate."

Cathy assumed, from the cat's injuries, that coyotes had attacked him. It's a fact of life for stray cats in a semi-rural area. It wasn't until much later that she learned that his wounds were neither accidental nor due to animals, but rather the deliberate action of a human being. Like the rest of the volunteers, her heart went out to Dodge. How could he be so friendly and trusting to members of the species that had harmed him so badly?

In the month that followed, Dodge's neck healed, his fur began growing back and his personality began to shine through the wreckage of his face. Regular meals put flesh back on his bones and they realized he was a very large, strong cat. "He had these huge pleading eyes that never failed to draw your attention," says Cathy. But beneath those eyes, a new problem was brewing. Dodge had developed a runny nose. Before long, despite medication and diligent nursing care, the seemingly minor cold had progressed to a thick mucous discharge that interfered with his breathing. Everyone at the shelter had become fond of Dodge by this time. They tried one thing after another, but by August, it was clear that nothing was working.

"My schedule changed considerably over the next few months and I was not in the centre as often as I used to be," says Cathy. But she kept tabs on Dodge, unable to forget about him.

A second set of skull x-rays showed that the metal fragments floating inside him had migrated into his sinuses, where they provided a perfect introduction for bacteria and infection. A draining track had formed from his sinuses into his mouth, his body's desperate attempt to fight the foreign material lodged in his tissues. Worse yet, laboratory tests showed that the infection was not caused by ordinary bacteria, but rather by super-bugs resistant to the usual antibiotics prescribed for such infections. His nose, his mouth, and even his ear had become inflamed and sensitive to the touch, indicating that the infection was spreading. Dodge was miserable; his caregivers were miserable.

Fortunately for Dodge, his injury was unusual enough to pique the interest of a board-certified feline dental specialist. Dr. Loic Legendre of Canada West Veterinary Specialists and Critical Care Hospital confirmed that the infected material in Dodge's head had to be removed. Because they'd be dealing with a tiny area snaked with hundreds of blood vessels, arteries, and crucial nerves, he recommended that the surgery be done at the referral hospital where they had the necessary equipment and trained support staff to perform such a delicate procedure. Although Dr. Legendre generously donated his surgery time, to help minimize costs, it was still far more than FVHS could afford.

"It was then that I offered to write a press release about him," says Cathy. "I'd never written one before and had no idea if I would get a response." She spent the next two nights writing and rewriting, then compiling a list of media contacts that might be interested in carrying Dodge's story.

"What happened next knocked me off my feet," says

Cathy. Newspapers, radio stations, and even television news broadcasts picked up his story. Dodge's handsome face was everywhere. "People opened up their hearts to him," she adds. In a matter of days, sufficient funds were raised, and on October 5th, Dodge went to Vancouver for surgery.

It was a grisly operation; in order to give Dodge's body a chance to begin healing, his entire nasal cavity had to be cleaned out. First Dr. Legendre incised down the middle of Dodge's nose. Then he very carefully picked out all the metal fragments he could find, as well as the damaged soft tissue. He also removed the contaminated bone and cartilage in the sinus cavity, hoping to eliminate the source of infection.

Then they sewed him back up and crossed their fingers. The next two weeks would be critical; Dodge needed a quiet environment, protected from sick cats that might pass on their illnesses to him. The shelter was not the best place for Dodge to convalesce. He needed a foster home, so Cathy and her husband Bernie volunteered to take him, hoping their own cats wouldn't complain too much! They were taught how to clean Dodge's incision and what to watch for as he healed.

The next morning Dodge, medicated with a "pain-patch," went to the Hamm home for his recovery. Aside from the swelling and stitches, the only sign of his invasive surgery was a slightly bloody nose. The other cats looked askance at this big, funny-looking cat with all the strange smells, but after some initial hissing and posturing, they contented themselves with black glares in his direction.

"We were ecstatic to watch Dodge make a complete recovery from his first surgery and admired him as he quickly returned to his usual happy-go-lucky friendly self," says Joyce Smith, corresponding secretary of the society. But they celebrated too soon; within a week of the surgery his nasty nasal discharge returned. Once more, he was put on antibiotics and once more, they were ineffective.

A disappointed Dr. Legendre advised a second, even more aggressive operation. This time, he planned to open up Dodge's nose completely and remove all the nasal turbinates (the convoluted bones and tissues that fill the inside of the nasal passage) in the left side of his nose. His news was not met with joy. How could a cat possibly enjoy a normal life after such a traumatic surgery? But Dr. Legendre assured them that this would be the best chance of removing all possible sources of infection once and for all. As for permanent side-effects, he told them that losing the cilia and filtering mechanisms on that side of his nasal cavity would probably leave Dodge prone to sneezing, and he might have a runny nose, but he would be otherwise healthy and comfortable.

In December, Dodge again went under the knife. Once Dodge was under anesthetic, the surgeons discovered that the infection had created a second draining track between his nose and mouth. This time, instead of approaching the problem through his nose, they went through his mouth.

All the teeth and surrounding bone and tissue on Dodge's upper left side were damaged beyond repair, and ruthlessly removed, the gums sewn back over the site. More dead tissue was scraped out of his nasal cavity. But this time, they recovered numerous metal fragments, the source of the infection, as well.

"We didn't know it then," says Cathy, "but Dodge would eventually have three surgeries. After the last one, he had a catheter tube temporarily implanted in his nose to administer antibiotics directly into the sinuses. It was just removed today and his vet is pleased with his progress."

Sometime between that first surgery and the last one, Cathy realized that she'd begun to think of Dodge as more than just a foster cat. But animal advocates cannot afford to fall in love with every creature that needs them. She steeled herself for the day that he'd go back to the shelter to await his permanent home. Then one day, she walked into her bedroom and found Dodge snuggled up with their other cats. If even their cats had changed their minds, and were willing to share their home with him, perhaps it was a sign. "He looked up at me with those big round eyes and that was it," Cathy admits. "I talked to Bernie and we agreed that Dodge had been through too much to uproot him again. He already had a forever home, right here with us."

"Dodge is a true gentle giant," Cathy adds. "It's amazing that despite everything he has been through, he still trusts and loves people."

CHAPTER

Take One Cat, as Needed, for Pain

"It is in their eyes that their magic resides."
—ARTHUR SYMONS

KNOCK, KNOCK.

The door eased open and Michelle Shaw peeked her head around the corner, into the room where a woman named Pat lay motionless with her head facing the wall, her eyes closed. This palliative care unit in Edmonton, Alberta, houses many different people. Some will stay for several weeks, others only a day or two, but the common factor is this: they are all dying, most of them from cancer.

Pat's family knew her time was fast approaching, and they'd gathered at her bedside to say their goodbyes, but Pat was no longer responding to anyone. The family, nervous and uncomfortable, didn't know what to do. That's when one of the therapists contacted Michelle to request a visit. There was no reason to expect that Michelle's presence would make any difference to Pat. But Michelle wasn't the reason for the request. Michelle's partner was—a small black cat named Ben.

Animal-assisted therapy had always intrigued Michelle, but it wasn't until Ben came into her life that the time was right to act on it. Many things contributed to her interest. Michelle was born with anatomical defects in both legs, a genetic condition that runs in her family. The bones in her upper and lower legs are angulated incorrectly, putting tremendous stress on the knee joints. She's had nine surgeries so far to correct the problem, but it will never be fixed completely. While medication usually controls her symptoms, there are days when the pain doesn't allow her to walk and nights when she's unable to sleep. A trained paralegal, Michelle now lives on disability income. "I think my chronic pain helps my work with palliative care," she says. "I understand loss of control. I understand not being able to do what you want, when you want."

But her understanding goes deeper than that. In 1987 Michelle graduated from high school, a driven student noted for her achievements. But the transition from high school to real life was a rude awakening. At the age of 20, while she was working as a receptionist at a Jasper ski resort, slowly but surely her world began to crack. She had a job, a place to live, and a roommate, but she was miserable. Her physical limitations hit home. Everything was harder than she'd expected. She was tired. She was lonely.

"They'd just done a show on *Oprah* on depression," says Michelle. "At the time I thought, 'man that sounds like me.' But I figured that probably half the viewers would be running to their doctors saying the same thing. It turns out that I should have gone running to my doctor."

The worst part was the black fog that swirled inside her brain. "I couldn't remember anything," Michelle says. "I couldn't remember the name of the place I worked sometimes. I couldn't remember if I'd taken the bus to work that day. One night a girlfriend phoned me to ask if I wanted to go out to dinner, and I had to go look for dirty dishes, because I couldn't remember if I'd already eaten."

She was devastated by what was happening to her. "When I graduated from high school, I won scholarships for top all-around student," she remembers. "Here I was supposed to be so smart, so full of promise and potential, and two years later, I couldn't remember my own name. It was humiliating." So Michelle took a bottle of pills and lay down, just wanting to fall asleep and never wake up. Except that she wasn't allowed to fall asleep.

Michelle and her roommate shared their place with a stray cat they'd named Toby. "He'd been hanging around, going in and out our window, and my roommate started feeding him," she says. Although he was technically her roommate's cat, Michelle and Toby developed a special bond. "We'd lie on the bed and he'd let me cry into the soft fur on his belly," she says. The cat sensed that Michelle needed him and on that night, he refused to let her push him away. "Every time I was just about to pass out, Toby screamed," Michelle recalls. "Oh my god, he screamed. I've never heard a noise like that. I'd pick him up, throw him out and he'd turn around and come back in and just SCREAM and scream and scream."

This went on all night. By dawn, Michelle knew her plan wasn't going to work. "I thought to myself, 'Geez, now you've done it. You're not going to kill yourself, but you're going to end up with brain damage.'" So she threw on a coat and walked the two blocks to Jasper's little hospital. She went straight to the Emergency Room doors, rang the bell, and then promptly fainted on the doorstep.

"I ended up in the intensive care unit in an Edmonton hospital," says Michelle. "I was lucky I didn't end up with kidney damage; I was just on the edge of having to go on dialysis." At the hospital, Michelle was forced to face the fact that she needed help, and she needed to make some changes in her life. Since her orthopedic specialists and now her psychiatrist were in Edmonton, she decided to move there herself, and Toby came with her. Counselling and medication got her life back on track. Michelle eventually got a job in a law office. She bought her first house.

She started thinking about pet therapy again, but she knew that only certain animals were right for the job. Despite the close bond she shared with Toby, she knew he wouldn't enjoy meeting new people in strange places. Plus, she wanted a kitten. She started watching the shelters, waiting for the right one to cross her path. "On November 1, 1997, nine years ago, I finally ended up with Ben, an SPCA special, who initially didn't seem right, either," says Michelle. In fact, not only did he seem wrong for pet therapy, he seemed positively possessed. While Michelle was at work during the day, Ben got into every sort of mischief imaginable. She never knew what sort of chaos she'd be returning to at the end of the day. "He'd drag raw steaks off the counter and across the carpet," she says. "He'd dig plants out by the roots." But worst of all was how he tormented Toby, leaping out at him from around corners, ambushing him from above. "He'd crawl on the back of Toby's shoulders when he was walking and cover his eyes with his paws," she remembers.

"Because he was so bad, I started taking him places with me after work, to give Toby a break," Michelle explains. "I'd take him with me to watch soccer games, for instance. And wouldn't you know it, out of the house, guess who was a perfect gentleman!" No one believed her when she described what a monster he was at home.

It made her think. Perhaps if Ben was capable of such good behaviour in public, he was suitable for pet therapy after all. That weekend, by chance, the *Edmonton Journal* ran a full-page spread about animal-assisted therapy. Michelle phoned the number for the Pet Therapy Society of Northern Alberta immediately. "They were so excited," she says, "because they always get requests for visits from cats but don't often have cats that can fill them."

They started training. Classes were held at the Cross Cancer Institute and a funeral home. Their group consisted of eight dogs, one rabbit, and Ben. "While we were going through training one day," says Michelle. "A young woman walked through, and she had a do-rag on her head, because she had no hair. I saw her and something just clicked. I knew that I wanted to do palliative care."

After a six-visit supervised practicum, Ben graduated from the program. "He got his scarf in February 1999!" says Michelle. "He wears his scarf whenever he's working so he knows what behaviour is expected of him." Ben seems to understand what the people he visits need, and that it's his job to comfort them. For instance, Ben has never let Michelle hold him close. "If I cuddle him he'll push away. Yet he'll let clients cuddle him. Even if I have a really bad migraine, and I think he'll know that I need him, nope. He won't let me," she explains. "The first time someone tried to cuddle him I began to say, 'No, he doesn't like it,' but he let them do it."

Since Michelle wanted to work with the dying, she and Ben had to do still more training at the hospice. Palliative care work can be draining, both emotionally and spiritually, but it is also tremendously rewarding. Michelle has never regretted her decision.

"It's a good thing," she says quietly. "When you're with these people who are dying, you learn that all that really matters is your loved ones and your faith. I've never once had people tell me about their jobs when they're dying."

Sometimes, it's a lesson in humility, too! When Michelle enters a room with Ben, all eyes go to the cat. Even when the patients talk with Michelle, it's Ben they're focussing on. "Recently I bumped into a woman I'd visited with Ben," she says with a laugh, "and the woman didn't recognize me at all, because he wasn't with me. Without the cat, they can't place me."

Michelle and Ben have several long-term care residents they visit regularly, particularly when they are on sabbatical from palliative care. Phyllis is a stroke victim they met while still in training. "She's very emotionally labile," says Michelle. "It's a common side effect of the stroke. All you have to do is ask, 'How are you?' and she'd start to cry. She can't control it. But after she's been with Ben for about 20 minutes she can actually talk before she starts to cry."

When Michelle and Ben began visiting Pat, Michelle knew the woman was near death. She'd stopped responding to both staff and visitors; it had been days since she'd last spoken. Nevertheless, Michelle knocked before entering, as she always does. "That room is their whole world," she emphasizes. "I knocked on her door, started to go in, and said, 'I'm Michelle, and this is Ben.'"

But that day, as they entered the room, Pat turned her head. She looked at Ben. Ben gazed back at her, and for one infinite moment, the two of them shared an unspoken mystical connection. Then Pat turned to Michelle, her eyes clear and focussed. She took a breath, opened her mouth and said, "I believe you." In this time of mortal reckoning, when the tangible things of this world fade in significance, Pat's words were stunning. "I didn't know what that meant," says Michelle, "but it was so profound, the way she said it, the way she looked at me."

In May of 2006, Michelle's experience with palliative care suddenly became personal, when she and Ben visited someone she'd met years ago, while working as a legal assistant. In 1998, Carol Ann, a high-functioning woman with a mental handicap, filed a lawsuit through Michelle's firm and Michelle was assigned to help on the case. "It was a big file and we spent a lot of time together," she recalls. They became friends. The case closed, Michelle changed law firms, but they kept in touch. "She'd always find me at Christmas and bring me a card," says Michelle. "But this Christmas, I didn't get a card." Then she got a phone call from the lawyer with whom she'd worked on Carol Ann's case. Carol Ann had cancer. She was dying. And she wanted to see Michelle.

It was a deeply touching request. "She only had hours or days left," says Michelle, "and she was asking for me! How flattering is that?" That same night, she went over to Carol Ann's home. "I sat and talked with her, although she was in and out because of the drugs," she says. "Then I asked if, when I came back the next day, she'd like me to bring a kitty?" Even in her weakened state, Carol Ann's enthusiasm was unmistakable. Then Michelle wondered if she'd spoken too quickly. Ben, after all, had never worked in a private home before. How would he react without nurses and hospital smells to remind him of his task?

By the next evening, Carol Ann's condition had deteriorated; Michelle was warned beforehand that her friend had slipped into a non-responsive state and might not even be aware of their presence. "I went anyway because of my personal belief that the patient can still hear you," says Michelle. When she and Ben entered the room, Carol Ann opened her eyes. She watched as Ben curled up on the bed beside her. She looked at the cat, and for a few minutes, the two of them shared an intense communication that transcended words, as if they were the only two souls in existence. "Then she looked at me and said, 'She knows.'" Because of his petite form, many of her clients assume Ben is a girl, Michelle explains. "I just said, 'Yes, she does.'" Carol Ann believed that Ben knew she was dying, and he was there to bring comfort to her.

Ben and Michelle sat with Carol Ann for four hours that evening, while the woman drifted in and out of consciousness, ever closer to her final breath. It was the longest Ben had ever spent visiting at one time. Carol Ann died a few days later.

Ben's calm gaze and warm body contain something no pill can match, and those that recognize it will do whatever they can to get their fill. Michelle brings a fleece blanket to all their visits, and where she puts it is where Ben is allowed to sit. "I tell you," says Michelle, "those palliative care people lie. I always ask them where it hurts, so I can make sure Ben doesn't go there. But they want to be as close as possible to the cat, so they don't tell me!"

"They love touch," she adds. "An animal has the ability to love unconditionally, despite physical disability or appearance. I think that's why it works." And for the patients, a little physical pain is well worth the emotional and spiritual comfort Ben brings.

7

A Real Man's Cat

"When you're special to a cat, you're special indeed . . .
she brings to you the gift of her preference of you, the sight
of you, the sound of your voice, the touch of
your hand." —LENORA FLEISCHER

DEEP IN ALBERTA'S EAST-CENTRAL farmland, 35 kilometres east of Edmonton, rests the little town of Ardrossan. The town boasts a colourful mix of those who make their living off the land as well as others who simply want to escape city life—professionals who are also hobby farmers, specialty livestock breeders, and woodworkers, office workers who ride rodeo or herd sheep on weekends. It's tough country, filled with resilient people who take pride in their ability to roll with the punches of a rich land that rewards muscle power and sweat.

Dave and Liz Hargreaves lived on a small country acreage in Ardrossan, where Dave worked as a senior technology analyst who acquired and managed state-of-the-art computer systems for Alberta Infrastructure and Transportation. Dave's daily life revolved around the technology with which the department maintained some 30,000 kilometres of provincial highways and over 137,000 kilometres of municipal roads. He dealt with everyone from politicians and corporate officials to farmers, ranchers, and construction workers. He knew about troubleshooting and problem solving. He understood the concrete, tangible aspects of day-to-day life. Then, in the fall of 1995, a certain little cat wandered into his life and introduced him to another side of himself.

"One warm October evening," says Dave, "we were enjoying a hamburger supper on our patio when I looked over to see this face staring at me." It was a stray cat, one they hadn't seen before. She was a pretty, multicoloured cat with dainty white paws. She delicately picked her way toward them with movements as precise and graceful as a dancer's and as Dave watched her, he felt something shift and stir inside him. Without even having touched her, he'd fallen under her spell.

Their own three cats, George, Torte, and Pussy Willows—a.k.a. PW—were not so enchanted. They immediately let the stranger know this was their territory and she was not welcome. But Dave and Liz, a palliative care nurse, felt sorry for her and suspected she was hungry. "We offered her some hamburger, but she shied away, because of the other cats," he says. Finally, despite PW's disgusted growls, she accepted a few bites of food. "I said, 'I think this cat's staying.' Liz said, 'I think so too.'"

But four cats? They already had more than enough cat hair in the house. What were they thinking? Their practical objections, however, couldn't compete with the sense that this was a cat that belonged with them. "There was something about her that pulled at my heart," admits Dave.

This was also a cat, however, who had learned the hard way to be cautious. After politely accepting the small meal, she deferred to the hostile glares coming from PW and disappeared into the night. Dave and Liz watched for her, secretly hoping she'd return, and a few days later she reappeared at the patio door. This time, instead of hunger and loneliness, she looked like she might have been injured. "Although she was very timid," recalls Dave, "she let me approach her and I picked her up for a closer look." One paw was swollen and obviously painful. They made an appointment to take her to the local veterinary hospital and, not ready to upset the other cats, settled her into the garage for the night.

The next day an examination revealed that not only was the paw indeed infected, but the little cat was also malnourished and infested with parasites. Dave suspected she'd been "dropped off" in the country and had perhaps lived for some time under the road in a drainage culvert. Within a few days, antibiotics and worm and mite treatments worked their miracles on her and she began to look healthier and happier. They named her Susie and accepted that they were now a four-cat family. PW, however, did not agree with Dave and Liz, and Susie took the opinions of PW very seriously. "She decided to take up residence in our garage where she ultimately spent the cold and snowy winter, refusing to come inside the house despite our many attempts," says Dave.

And thus began a morning ritual: Dave brought fresh food, chipped away at the ice that had formed on her water dish and scratched her behind the ears before setting off for work. It wasn't long before she took to following him around the house and grounds. After all, he still had daily tasks to attend to. Responsible men didn't waste time petting cats. But Susie didn't mind. When he shovelled snow late at night, she was there; as he walked ankle deep in snow to the wood-shed, she would follow, hopping first into and then out of his icy footsteps. One time as he climbed up onto the roof of the house to adjust the television antenna, he discovered as he turned to come down that she'd climbed the ladder and waded through the snow to come and "help" him.

As winter turned to spring and summer, Susie became friendlier and braver, eventually even coming into the house now and then. PW, old and grumpy, did not take kindly to this and many times they came to blows, fighting fiercely on the living room floor. Torte, the tortoiseshell, also disliked Susie, but chose to ignore her whenever pos-sible rather than fight. George didn't mind Susie, but chose to stay well away when it looked like she and PW were about to get into a serious altercation. Susie had learned that this home was now her home, and although she often stood her ground with old PW, it was dogs she hated, fiercely attacking them until they left howling.

As summer turned to autumn and then winter again, Dave finally convinced Susie to move from the garage into her own suite in the basement. Each night, as he fed the others, Susie sat patiently waiting on the sidelines in her segregated corner, her large eyes watching carefully and always those two white paws neatly tucked together.

In the spring of 1998, privatization changed the face of Dave's career and took them from Alberta to the West Coast. George had passed away the previous winter, but Dave and Liz had to make arrangements to get the other three out to their new home. Given that Susie and PW couldn't even be in the same room together, it was a tricky situation. Finally they hit upon a solution. "Torte and PW travelled with us in the car while Susie was to stay behind with Liz's daughter Jennifer until we were settled in our new home, when Dave and Liz would fly her out," he says.

They had bought property on Pender Island in the Gulf Islands, and made plans to build their dream home. Surrounded by old-growth forest and abundant wildlife, it was the idyllic setting they'd always imagined. But Dave still had to work in Victoria; he thought at first that he could commute, but they soon realized that their dream would have to be put on hold for a bit longer. In the interim, they were to move house several times and each time the cats would be forced to adjust to a new neighbourhood and new dangers. "One house in particular was on a busy street in Victoria where Susie would often stroll across the street to explore," recalls Dave. "We worried that she would get killed, but her road sense was strong and although she liked to explore the neighbourhood, she never strayed far from home."

In the spring of 2000, age and infirmity finally got the better of old PW. The following year, Dave took early retirement and he and Liz gathered Susie and Torte and took them to their new home off the wild west coast of British Columbia. "The adventures of Gulf Island living fascinated Susie," says Dave. "Her occasional hunting trips would yield mice, salamanders, and even the occasional snake, often to be deposited in our living room or bedroom as an obvious 'gift.' It was amusing to see the first snake she caught wrapped around her nose."

The fast world of highways and hard science was over for Dave. Now his life revolved around quieter island activities. "I actually got involved in carpentry, doing house renovations and finishing work," he says. "Having spent my working life at a desk, it was good to get out and do physical stuff. There's something about working with wood that soothes the soul." But he didn't stop there; he even joined a local poetry group. He listened mostly, enjoying the magic of a well-chosen word and the courage of those who chose to share their work.

Dave found that their new lifestyle suited him. Susie loved the fact that Dave was always around now. When he and Liz went outside for their walks, Susie often followed them down the road. Susie had made friends with the neighbours nearby, especially Jackie and Erik, who cared for the cats when Dave and Liz went away. Susie often walked over to visit, knowing a friendly pat and a dish of food would be there for her.

Like most old cats, she loved to sleep. Her favourite sleeping spot was on Dave and Liz's bed, between the two pillows, often with her head on one of them, softly purring until she got too hot and left for the cooler space by the door. She also liked high places, particularly house roofs, and many times Dave found her looking down from this high perch, amazed that she could still make her way up there. Whenever Dave went up to clean the moss off their low-slope roof, Susie followed him. "One of the last times she was up on the roof she had trouble getting down," he says. She tried to clamber down and ended up falling the last little way. After that, Dave always checked to see if she'd climbed up after him and waited to help her down.

But eventually, she even stopped that. Instead of accompanying Dave and Liz on their walks, she patiently waited for their return on the side of the road. They'd had her for 12 years at that time. The veterinarian estimated her age at five or six years when she first came to them. Susie was now an old cat. "You sort of realize that the day's going to come when you're going to have to lose her," says Dave.

In the fall of 2004 they noticed her ribs were more prominent than they should be. They looked more closely but the truth was unavoidable. Susie had lost weight. They tempted her appetite with all manner of treats and delicacies, but it made no difference. A veterinary exam revealed some dental problems, so they had her teeth cleaned. It perked her up for a little while, but before long, she was picking at her food again. She kept getting thinner and just before Christmas, they learned why: a large, inoperable tumour in her abdomen. "We'd often thought about what we would do when the day finally came that Susie would leave us," says Dave, "but no amount of preparation can ease the pain of the loss of a pet. When it happens, you feel like your whole world is falling apart."

Although she grew steadily weaker and weaker, she stubbornly continued going out for short walks, sometimes even visiting Jackie and Erik next door. When she was too tired, she simply sat on the front porch, watching the world go by. During the last days of her life, she continued slowly picking her way over the snowy ground, determined to go next door one more time. "One cold night, I found her sitting at their door—they had gone away—looking up to be let inside," says Dave. "She had no way of knowing they weren't there."

Susie lasted until January 17 when, too sick and weak to move far, it was obvious that her time had come. With trembling voice, Dave called the vet to make her final appointment. "We broke down and cried buckets for days after that," remembers Dave. Even Liz, who dealt with death on a daily basis, was astounded at the sense of loss Susie's passing stirred in them. "Perhaps the hardest part of all," says Dave, "was when we placed her in the box I had made for her, screwed on the lid and placed it in the ground."

Dave had never experienced such grief before and he didn't know how to cope with the volume of feeling Susie's death dredged up. "I come from a generation where it's not a manly thing to show your emotions," he explains. "It's okay when your parents die or your kids or something drastic happens. But with animals it's not." He spent a great deal of time reflecting on how Susie's life and death had affected them in such a lasting way. He decided to try and express it through poetry. "As soon as I started writing, it just flowed," he says. "When stuff hurts like that it's easy to do." But could he be brave enough to share his words with others at the local poetry group? It was a huge risk, one he'd never have taken in his other life. "I felt that people here in the Gulf Islands are freer to open up and show their emotions," he says. "Guys on the oil patch wouldn't think much of it."

So, he reached down into himself for courage, took a deep breath, stood up, and read his poem to the group. "This was within a month or two of her dying," he says. "It's a tough thing to share something that emotional, without breaking down. They picked up on that and were very supportive." Often, when people share experiences that are deeply emotional, it's difficult for others to know how to respond. "People don't know what to say," explains Dave. "It's like when you visit someone who is sick or dying. You think, 'What do I do? What do I say?' But you don't have to do anything. You just have to be there."

Be there. Listen. It's a simple lesson, and Susie mastered it. "Animals give us unconditional love," Dave adds. "We're all looking for unconditional love and when you suddenly lose it like this, the pain can touch the soul of the strongest of us."

This is his poem:

What is this thing you do to me
When on my knees I weep for thee.
"What is so bad?" they say to me. "Animals die all the
*   time."*
And real men are not supposed to cry.
It hurts that you now don't follow me,
And I don't trip or step on your tail.
I should be glad you don't hinder me,
And my task in a man's world can easier be
Because real men are not supposed to cry.
My days are grey and tears do fall,
I blame the weather and the rain and all,
Yet in my heart a hole has grown where once your
*   paw would often fall.*
And I am torn because
Real men are not supposed to cry.

A Real Man's Cat

As a man I found the strength to do,
This I knew I had to do
I stayed with you until the end and held you tight as
my best friend.

And I learned that real men can sometimes cry.

This grief today has helped me see
That through your eyes it had to be.
I thank you for your life and love and for teaching me
that . . .

It is okay for men to cry . . .

CHAPTER

8

When Business Goes to the Cats

"One cat just leads to another." —ERNEST HEMINGWAY

IN LANGLEY, BRITISH COLUMBIA, A tiny store peeks out from beneath a weathered awning in the downtown Salt Lane district, an unexpectely retro part of an otherwise ordinary city. The sun drenched one-way street is reminiscent of small-town markets in days gone by, but the upscale merchants definitely cater to tourists and shoppers of the new millennium. Authentic African art, custom-designed jewellery, and antiques nestle cheek-by-jowl with a fresh seafood store, tanning salon, and a paint-your-own ceramics outlet. When customers are finished shopping, the aromas of coffee and fresh baking lead them to sit down and take a break.

But perhaps the most unusual business is Kitty Kingdom,

whose motto is "Where Cats Rule!" Long-time cat-lover Davena Tarkanen, owner and operator of Kitty Kingdom, has made it her business to know what cats and cat lovers want and to provide it for them. Walking through the tinkling front door, browsers are immediately inundated with everything they could imagine—and a few things they'd never thought of—from the usual mugs decorated with every shape and colour of cat to interestingly padded tea cozies with tails, and custom-made jewellery and watches with whiskers and ears. Elaborate scratching posts and climbing trees fill the front window. Next to them rest miniature hammocks and handcrafted beds, for what does any cat want more than a comfy place to sleep? If there's anything a collector of feline paraphernalia covets, Davena either has it or knows where to get it. Cats really do rule in this store.

There were always cats in her childhood home, deep in the remote wilderness off the tip of Vancouver Island. Her mother wasn't particularly enthusiastic, recalls Davena, but children are persistent and she finally gave in, allowing them to have one cat, a male, so there would be no chance of kittens. Over the years, however, the one-cat rule was bent considerably. "One of the first cats I really remember having as a kid was a stray cat named Smokey, who just showed up at our house one day," she says. "We never were able to find his rightful owner, so we were allowed to keep him. He was a fantastic cat." He put up with a lot from Davena and her sister. "We were pretty young at the time and we liked to play dress-up with Smokey," she recalls. "Sometimes he would wear doll clothes. He probably didn't like it, but he never retaliated! We had Smokey for about five years and then he just disappeared one day and we never saw him again."

Davena's childhood had few luxuries and likewise her cats had to make do with what they got. "The nearest vet was a ferry ride and then about a five-hour drive away, so our cats weren't neutered," says Davena. She remembers hearing spectacular fights, especially during mating season. While these fights were brutal on the cats, they served to fill in a few gaps in Davena's knowledge of biology. "I remember one time my sister and I went outside at night in our pyjamas to break up what we thought was a cat fight on our roof that really wasn't a cat fight," she says, smiling. "I think it was during times like these that one of our cats really did have nine lives."

Irving was a particularly small cat, whose size was a distinct disadvantage in the world of catfights. "Irving came home pretty beat up a few times," says Davena. She recalls one harrowing time when Irving came home with his tail soaked in some kind of oil. He'd tried to clean himself off, naturally, and became very ill as a result. "It was nerve-wracking doing what you could and hoping for the best. He barely ate for days and I remember spoon feeding him food that was pretty watered down to get him eating." Irving recovered, luckily, but Davena is glad that today, all her cats have easy access to medical care if needed. "As an adult who lives in the city," she says, "I really enjoy being able to drive a few blocks to a vet as well as having 24-hour emergency veterinarians available!"

Other than a brief period in her early adult life, Davena has never been without cats. "I worked as a commercial fisher and was away for about six months of the year," she says. "After I quit fishing, I settled down and had my son, and we adopted our first cat." Dragon, who is still with them today, was born to a stray cat, under the porch of an abandoned house. An acquaintance rescued them, had the mother spayed, and cared for the kittens until they found homes. "These kittens were pretty wild, but our kitten followed my four-year-old son around on their farm and we knew we would have to adopt her," says Davena. "We had been chosen." Another four-year-old had christened the kitten Dragon, and the adoption hinged on the name staying unchanged, so Dragon she remained. "Although she hissed at us occasionally, and hid behind and under things, she warmed up quickly and became a wonderful pet." Dragon, now 11 years old, originally followed Davena's son around, but has since become Davena's cat. "She's claimed my king-sized bed as her own!" she says. Dragon doesn't even let their other cats, George and Lance, in the room, much less on the bed.

Cats are in Davena's blood. "Both my sister and I collected cat paraphernalia and it was when trying to find unique gifts for her—and myself—that I first thought it would be great if someone would open such a shop," Davena says. The thought that perhaps that "someone" would be her didn't come until much later, when she was working as webmaster for a tele-communications company. She often chatted with a fellow co-worker who also loved cats and the conversation invariably turned to what neat item they'd recently seen and where they could get it. "I really don't remember the first time I thought about doing this," says Davena. "I kept saying, 'Somebody really should open a store just for cats and cat lovers,' but I didn't think that someone would be me for a long time!"

Then she was laid off from her job. Suddenly, the world had offered her an opportunity, but she wasn't sure exactly what to do with it. She began to investigate possible ways to turn her existing knowledge and interests into a viable business. That's when the seed of idle chat began to take root. Her husband, Rob, encouraged her to follow her heart. "He's a total cat lover," she says with a smile. "We got married eight years ago and I knew he was the one for me when he talked baby-talk to my cat. That did it."

After some research, Davena found that, while there were mail-order stores that offered cat-related items, most were in the United States. "There were certainly none in Canada that offered a good selection of products both for cat lovers and their cats," she says. "Many Canadians don't want to order from the United States due to added costs for duty." Plus, she suspected many Canadians would prefer to support a Canadian business, if they had the option.

Through Internet forums and surveys, she continued gathering data. The idea of a cat store had taken root, but the only way she could go ahead with it was if she had solid evidence that it could be financially viable. Banks don't lend money for passion alone. The response was overwhelming; she identified a large number of people who indicated they would be interested in shopping at such a store and the numbers, Davena felt, might be exponentially higher. "Cat lovers know other cat lovers," says Davena. So, the idea had legs. But was it enough for a "real" store? Could she invest their savings and borrow money for this? The majority of small businesses fail in the first year, especially when run by inexperienced owners and when they appeal to a highly specialized niche market.

She decided there was a way to start off slowly, minimize the risks, and get a better feel for the demand. She put her Web design training to work and created a virtual store, where customers could browse an extensive inventory of toys, supplies, and collectibles and order on-line. She called her fledgling business CAT-alog.

"The CAT-alog.com site was designed and developed in-house, with the help of my three cats: Dragon, George and Lance," says Davena. "Special mention should go out to Dragon, who is performing intensive product testing at the moment." Dragon, the reigning queen of the company, insisted on being involved in every step of the development of CAT-alog.com, perching on Davena's desk and trotting across the keyboard.

Davena also puts them to use on the Quality Assurance team; every new cat toy is thoroughly tested by Davena's trio before getting the nod. "The pictures on our site show the cats hard at work!" says Davena. "When the cats aren't busy testing products, they can be found underfoot or sleeping in one of their many comfy kitty hideaways."

CAT-alog officially opened for business in November 2003, and orders immediately started flooding in. To make sure she could fill them quickly, Davena's inventory grew steadily larger and larger. "Soon, I'd filled every closet, every nook and cranny, the shed, the rec room," she recalls. "I was moving five things to get to one."

In those early days, Davena and Rob spent many weekends at cat shows, sitting behind their booth, promoting CAT-alog. "Rob's been a huge help by coming to the shows with me and helping with set-up, tear-down, and product sales at all of the shows we have attended," emphasizes Davena. Not surprisingly, sales skyrocketed at these events where people could actually pick up and touch items. "Although it was expensive travelling to shows, this was a great way to meet cat lovers and get our name out."

The face-to-face experience bolstered her confidence. Perhaps there was a market for a "real" store. By the summer of 2005, it wasn't a matter for thought anymore; there was no room in her house. She had to take her business into the real world. In November 2005, Kitty Kingdom was born. CAT-alog orders still come in, but now they're filled from behind the cash register where Davena can also meet customers in the flesh.

The line between work and play is blurred these days and she wouldn't have it any other way. In her spare time, she helps various cat rescue coalitions by building and maintaining Web sites. "I'm very interested in seeing people become more responsible cat owners," she says. "I try to help where I can to improve living conditions for abandoned and stray cats by doing volunteer work for local cat shelters." Such behind-the-scenes work is vital to the survival of rescue organizations and the cats they rescue.

For Davena, Kitty Kingdom and the CAT-alog business is the perfect combination of cats, people, and business. "There's one woman who comes in every Saturday, faithfully. She picks up a treat for her cat and maybe something for herself. I don't want to miss her!" Davena knows how lucky she is to be able to earn a living doing what she loves. "I don't think I could be in just any retail," she admits. "But I can talk about cats all day."

9

Tiger's Lucky Toes

"Her function is to sit and be admired."
—GEORGINA STRICKLAND GATES

AT THE LEDUC PICTURE STORE in Leduc, Alberta, near Edmonton, a small cat named Tiger sits near the front door. A customer comes in, stoops to stroke Tiger, then approaches the man at the counter. "Can you take a picture of me with her?" she asks. Garth Ukrainetz, owner of both store and cat, smiles and reaches for the camera. He's used to this. Tiger is well known in Leduc and even people from out of town come to see her and get a photo with the famous cat. Tiger graciously poses with the woman, accepts some more attention and compliments, and goes back to her job as official greeter.

What makes Tiger so special? Well, as cat lovers know, all cats are special in their own way. Garth, his wife

Coralee, and their daughter Cassandra would say that Indiana, Rocky, and Squeaker, their other cats, are just as deserving, but they can't deny that Tiger has something other cats don't have. Several somethings, in fact. Instead of 18 toes—five on each front foot and four on each back foot—Tiger boasts 27, seven on each front foot and one back foot and six on the other back foot.

Polydactyly, Greek for "many fingers," is a fairly common mutation in the domestic feline world and has a variety of expressions. It may simply be an enlargement of the inside digit into a thumb (known as a "mitten cat"), or it may take the mild form of one extra toe on a single paw. It may show up as one extra toe on each paw or, in more extreme cases, there may be several additional fully formed toes on any or all of the paws.

Tiger's feet are part of what drew Garth and Coralee to her in the first place. On a cold snowy January day in 2001, a mother cat lay curled up in her bed, exhausted. She'd just given birth to four kittens. They nestled against her warm grey sides, kneading the soft flesh as they suckled eagerly. One kitten, the only girl, was considerably smaller than the rest. But her diminutive limbs carried paws that looked like they belonged on a much larger cat.

Though the condition varies from animal to animal, it always affects the front feet and sometimes the back feet as well. Although it is technically considered a deformity, most polydactyl cats are not disabled and have no problems with balance or in walking, climbing, and jumping. Because the extra toes are often a different length than the other toes, polydactyl cats can have claws that grow unevenly, making it hard for the cats to wear them down with their ordinary nail-sharpening activities. If the extra claws are allowed to grow unchecked, they can actually curl around and grow right back into the paw pad. Regular nail trims are a must for these cats!

Sometimes, two extra toes are fused together, which also fuses the nail bed, leading to the growth of one "superclaw." Stronger and thicker than normal claws, these superclaws can be lethal to furniture and human flesh, making routine nail trims even more important. Tiger has a couple of these fused claws but has never had trouble because of them.

"When we took her from her mama, a blue Persian with 24 toes, her feet were huge. I counted her toes when we arrived home and was amazed to find that she had 27," says Garth. But he didn't think much more of it at the time. When Garth and Coralee first got Tiger, they were living in an apartment where pets were not allowed and he was afraid she'd be found out. So rather than leave her alone, Garth took Tiger with him to work at their picture framing shop every morning. "I used to gently stuff her in my coat when I left the apartment so no one would see her," he says. "She was really good from the start, she didn't squirm or cry out when I hid her in my jacket." Tiger still likes to go for drives in the car. "She sits on my shoulder and watches the world go by as we drive," Garth adds. "She has no fear of driving like most cats do. In the wintertime she's like a warm scarf."

Tiger loved to hang out in the quiet store, wandering among the displays and looking at the new prints hanging on the walls. Mostly though, whether at work or home, Tiger loves to be near Garth. "When I am watching TV on the couch she always climbs on top of me and has a snooze. When I'm sleeping in bed she climbs on top, too. When I am eating she'll jump up on my shoulder and sit there. When I'm at work she is always near."

One day a man came into the store and, after receiving the usual Tiger-greeting, looked more closely at the little cat's feet. He mentioned to Garth that he'd never seen so many toes on one cat before and they should consider contacting Guinness World Records. "So I did," says Garth. "After much scrutinizing, on December 12, 2001, Tiger was awarded world record status by the Guinness people in England, as 'the cat with the most toes.'"

Tiger beat out the previous record holder, Twinkle Toes, owned by Gloria Boensch of Birch Run, Michigan. The three-year-old female has a mere 25 toes. She has received a certificate verifying her distinction. So until recently, when an Ontario cat with 28 toes displaced her, all Guinness World Record Attractions museums featured a display about Tiger.

The recognition created a flurry of media attention over Tiger from around the world. She was featured in magazines, on television programs, in newspaper articles, and on the radio. "Tiger the '27-Toed Cat' is a famous little celebrity in the Edmonton area," says Garth. "She has helped raise money for a few local charities." But thankfully, the celebrity hasn't gone to her head. Ironically, all the TV and newspaper attention eventually alerted their landlord to their illegal tenant and they were evicted. But the couple, looking forward to starting their family, was planning to move anyway and who wants to live in a place that doesn't welcome cats?

"One thing I have to say about Tiger is that she is calm, cool, and collected. She doesn't freak out like other cats do." She also does "toe paintings," which Garth sells at his shop. "Many people come to my shop just to see Tiger and take pictures with her."

Polydactyl cats have always attracted an inordinate amount of attention and various myths and folk tales have grown up around them as a result. Legend has it that cats with extra toes were sought after by pirates to keep on their ships, because cats with extra toes were thought to be lucky. The reputation likely grew out of the belief that their large paws made them exceptionally good mousers, which would certainly be a desirable trait on a ship. Pirate ships, merchant marines, and naval vessels all needed cats to control rodents and if they had extra toes, so much the better! When these seamen settled back on land, their cats often stayed with them, which helps to explain the high incidence of polydactyl cats along the North American east coast. At one time,

40 percent of the original population of Maine Coon cats in New England were polydactyl. The cold winters in this area led to claims that the cats developed extra toes to act as snowshoes. There is also a high incidence of polydactyl cats on the other side of the "pond" in southwest England, perhaps for the same sea-faring reason.

Boston, Massachusetts, is in fact the epicentre of multi-toed cat distribution. When biologists examined various cities with high populations of polydactyl cats, they found that this occurrence is directly linked to a human population with high numbers of ex-Bostonians. Cats with extra toes, they decided, were reflecting human cultural movement!

Polydactyl cats have friends in high places. President Teddy Roosevelt had one named Slippers. Writer Ernest Hemingway, a great cat lover, had numerous polydactyl cats among the dozens that shared his island. One, named Princess Six Toes, was a favourite of photographers and appeared in the *New York Times* and other American magazines. Hemingway's notoriety has forever linked him to multi-toed cats; many people even refer to them as "Hemingway cats."

Tiger may have held the record, but other cats have had their moment in the spotlight. In 1978, a purebred Siamese named Big Foot, owned by Miss Joan Conerly of Wauchula, Florida, was reported to have had 26 toes, seven on each front paw and six on each back paw. Big Foot's family illustrates the strength of this inherited trait: Big Foot's mother had 22 toes, one of his sisters had 22 toes, and one of his brothers had 24 toes.

To date, the greatest number of toes ever found on a cat is an incredible 32, eight on each paw, reported in October 1974, on a cat called Mickey Mouse, owned by Renee Delgade of Westlake Village, California. It is possible he had double-paws, a condition in which each paw is actually two fused mirror image paws; this is different from polydactyly. The condition, also seen in humans, appears as a central thumb with four fingers to either side, making a natural baseball catcher's glove. When a cat with four double-paws sits "at attention," he appears to have eight paws, all in a row. Similar to polydactyly, this condition is a developmental defect. Very early in cell division, instead of forming a normal limb, the tip of the limb bud splits, producing two mirror-image paws on the same leg, set at right angles to each other.

But even stranger things have happened. In 1976, a female cat named Triple, owned by Mr. and Mrs. Bertram Bobnock of Iron River, Michigan, was documented as having 30 toes, but, unlike the polydactyl and double-pawed cats, Triple's toes were arranged on six paws, located on five legs! Her left hind leg reportedly split at the hock, growing into two complete lower legs. One of those lower legs had two paws. This was probably due to a developmental defect, which caused the growing tip of the limb bud to split, but still allowed each part of the fork to develop into a limb. The fork would have occurred twice, once at the hock and then a second time on one side when it would have forked again to grow the paw.

Tiger sits quietly on Garth's shoulder even if he's walking through a crowd of thousands of noisy people. "I used to take her down to the Edmonton Fringe Festival and walk around with her on my shoulder," he says. "She likes to people-watch."

She also likes to watch hockey on TV. "I think she's fascinated with watching the hockey puck move all around the ice," Garth says. "Whenever the Edmonton Oilers make the hockey playoffs, I take Tiger down to the stadium before the game, in the hope that her good luck will rub off on the Oilers." Unfortunately, it doesn't always work. Even Tiger's luck wasn't enough for the Oilers in Game 7 of the 2006 series. But the occasional miss doesn't worry Garth. He's still a believer. "Do I think Tiger has brought good luck to our household?" Garth muses. "Yes! More importantly, Tiger brings playfulness and love to our family."

10

Kitty's Song

"A cat does not want all the world to love her . . . only those she has chosen to love." —HELEN THOMSON

OH DANNY BOY, THE PIPES, *the pipes are calling . . .*
In the spring of 1993, Steve Perli sat in his hatchback at the end of the gravel road as the last light of day faded into greyness. *The summer's gone and all the flowers are dying . . .* The mournful melody ran through his head again and again, drowning out the rowdy pub songs he'd once sung with a laughing, Irish-eyed woman. Now instead of promises of love, all he had were memories, mist, and sadness, the landscape of his heart. Grey sky, grey road, grey life. "This is it," he thought. "I've taken as much as I can bear." All he wanted was one reason to live. After nearly five decades, was that too much to ask? Apparently it was. Not a single soul, he realized, would miss the solitary night

watchman in his isolated life. His hands felt far away from his body as he lifted the muzzle of his .30-30 Winchester rifle and slowly turned it toward his head. It was time. He closed his eyes. *Oh Danny boy . . .*

Thud!

His eyes flew open, the gun lurched in his hands, and he automatically took his finger off the trigger. There, on his windshield, looking pleadingly through the glass directly into his eyes, crouched a cat. In one endless moment, the world outside disappeared and everything focussed in on that shining pinpoint where their eyes met. Steve's heart thumped in his chest and a rushing sound filled his ears. With shaking hands he lowered the gun, unwilling to complete the act in view of this silent witness.

Like a jostled phonograph needle, his mind jumped from the track it had been stuck on for so long, skipped to a new song. He'd seen this cat before, but where? Then he remembered: a few weeks earlier, he'd been wandering through a nearby livestock barn during a horse auction. He ducked away from the bustling crowds, preferring to walk past the stalls, admiring the animals, when a thin, tortoise-shell tabby cat streaked across the breezeway in front of him. Steve had barely paid any attention to her, but now he wondered if she was the same cat he'd seen skulking around the buildings he guarded as night watchman.

Perched on the hood of his car, she was even thinner than she'd been when he'd caught his first glimpse of her.

Luminous amber eyes stood out hugely in her gaunt face. Although she watched him with justifiable caution, she appeared willing to give him the benefit of the doubt, as if she knew that sometimes people were friendly.

She'd been dumped, Steve guessed. He'd seen it before; people found a quiet road on the outskirts of town, looked both ways before opening the door and setting kitty "free." Free to starve. Free to be killed by coyotes or hit by a car. Free to shiver through the winter in fear and loneliness, with nothing to hope for but a quick release from a loveless life.

"Poor thing," he thought, as they eyed each other guardedly through the windshield. "I know just how you feel."

Steve had been a loner all his life. His childhood in Ontario was scarred by complicated family relations and a father with quick fists. School was no better than home; although gifted with a brilliant mind, behavioural tics made Steve a social disaster, a pariah among his peers. Today, such students are assessed, diagnosed, and provided with special assistance to help them succeed. In Steve's day, they were labelled, laughed at, and left to stumble along as best they could.

Nevertheless, he grew up and went out on his own. He became certified as a mechanic and for the next 30 years, travelled extensively. With his skills, work was easy to find and he favoured the hot places, like Arizona, Nevada, and Mexico. He picked up languages easily, eventually becoming fluent in Spanish, German, and French. He listened to country-and-western music, collected autographs of celebrities, and once even met Marilyn Monroe in person.

But relationships with people remained a problem. Steve had long ago stopped expecting anything but criticism or rejection and, like many frightened, lonely people, had learned to protect himself by striking the first blow. Finally, too much alcohol and too many years of hard living caught up with him. He found himself in British Columbia's Fraser Valley and there, not yet an old man, he suffered a mild stroke. It was the last straw; the disappointments of his life came crashing down on him. He'd made the decision to end it all when the little cat interrupted him.

Steve set the gun on the backseat and began searching his car for something to offer his small guest. He emerged with nothing more than a couple of coffee creamers, but these he poured into a plastic lid and set before her. She lapped them up daintily and then looked at him as if to say, "Now what?" He reached out a hand and when she didn't flinch, he patted her apologetically and wished her well. Then he drove back to his shack and put the Winchester safely up onto the rack, his grim plan firmly tucked away in the back of his mind. It was time for bed. Tomorrow would be a new day.

Mrrow!

The sound pulled him from the misty depths of sleep and he fumbled for the light switch. The sudden glow illuminated a grisly scene and he blinked in confusion. His rustic one-room home had only the bare essentials, but it was usually free of dead bodies. Not tonight. The little cat had found her way into his cabin and brought with her a thank-you gift: a freshly killed mouse.

"I don't eat mice," Steve told her crossly. "You eat it!" And she did.

He turned out the light, shifted deeper beneath the blankets and closed his eyes again. Darkness enfolded him and he faded back into sleep.

Mrrow!

For the second time, he bolted up in bed, grabbing at the light switch. The cat had brought him a tiny dead bunny. She sat with her prize between two tidy feet, looking at him expectantly.

"I don't eat bunny either," Steve told her, but less crossly this time. "You eat it." And she did.

When morning came, Steve remembered the past day's events as if in a dream. Had he really almost killed himself? Had he really been interrupted at the last moment by a stray cat? As he clumsily prepared his simple breakfast, he doubted himself. There was no cat, he told himself. He probably made it all up because he was a coward, too afraid to take the final step. He felt himself slip into the same familiar despondency that had so long plagued him.

Then, through a small hole in the shack's dilapidated door, he saw a face, big eyes in a bony head.

Mrrow!

There she was! She was real and she was back. She

walked toward him on dainty paws, her tail waving gracefully above her slender back. When she reached his side, she stopped and looked up at him, as if she'd finally found what she'd been searching for. Perhaps, Steve thought with slow-dawning awe, she needed him. Maybe she actually wanted to be with him. Steve hadn't felt needed or wanted in a very long time.

Steve pushed up his sleeves and went to look through his boxes and bags for something a cat might enjoy. He couldn't kill himself now, he told himself. He had a cat to look after.

The next time he went to the grocery store, he threw some tinned cat food into his basket. He didn't know what the kitty liked, so he got some of everything: beef in gravy, chicken in gravy, veal in gravy. She ate whatever he offered, neatly polishing the plate with her raspy tongue before settling down for a good wash.

Although she appeared willing to settle in, after a couple of days, Steve noticed something peculiar. Each day, as afternoon stretched into evening, the little cat stationed herself at the cabin door, listening to the cars going by on the road beyond them. Now and then she jumped up and ran down the drive, only to return slowly and dejectedly some time later. After he'd watched her do the same thing several times, Steve suddenly knew what was wrong. She was waiting for someone, a familiar engine sound that would bring the people she loved back to her. Surely one of the cars that she recognized would be "her" car, come to take her home again.

Poor thing, Steve thought again. She could wait and hope all she wanted, but they were never coming back for her.

"You've been dumped, Kitty," he told her, remembering the Irish pub nights. "Just like me. Best get over it and get on with your life."

Kitty eventually stopped waiting to be reclaimed and turned her energy to making a life with Steve. It wasn't until months later that he realized with astonishment that he no longer thought about his date with the Winchester. In fact, he hadn't thought about death at all. He was too busy living. The painful memories were still there, but he wasn't alone in his pain anymore. He had Kitty now. They had each other.

There was no way to know how long Kitty had been on her own. Although she was clearly an accomplished hunter, Steve wondered how hungry she'd got before she learned to fend for herself. When Kitty had been with him for about three months, she showed him. One of the businesses he looked after, a concrete factory, stored railroad ties in part of the lot. Stacked cross-wise, these formed a sort of cave. One evening on their rounds, Kitty walked toward them, then sat down and looked at Steve, waiting for him to follow her.

"I'm coming, I'm coming," he told her, curious. She leaped up again and trotted into the "cave" and climbed up inside. Steve crouched beneath the ties and peered up to where Kitty had disappeared. She popped her head out, beckoning him to come further. Deep within he found a lair, littered with bones. This, then, was where she'd set up base camp after her abandonment. She was a survivor! And she trusted him enough to share her secret place with him.

But what warmed Steve's heart was the knowledge that Kitty didn't need him because she was *physically* starving; it was companionship she'd craved. She didn't stay with Steve because he fed her; she chose to live with him simply because she liked him.

Their days together took on a comfortable rhythm. Simple tasks, shared solitude. When it came time to make his nightly rounds, he whistled for the little cat and she came bounding to accompany him. *Oh Danny Boy* . . . now the whistled Irish melody held notes of comfort to him, new memories and a shared grief overcome. Together, they went from one door to another, checking locks and peering into windows, looking for intruders. If anything was amiss, Kitty warned Steve with anxious chatter and tail-flicking.

She also began expressing, ever so politely, her food preferences. "What do you want for supper?" Steve asked every day, gesturing to the shelves laden with the various options. Kitty reached up with one graceful paw and tapped at the shelf with her favourite: veal in gravy. If he was out of that one, she'd tap her next favourite. If they were down to the last few cans, she'd deign to eat the chicken in gravy, but only until the next shopping trip.

And so they passed the next 12 years, in quiet seclusion, two broken hearts taking solace in each other.

The first time Jim Matthies saw Steve, he recognized that this was a man on the fringe of society. The shack Steve lived in was on the property of the trucking company Jim worked for; the company allowed Steve rent-free accommodations, such as they were, in exchange for his service as a security guard. The solitude and rough living didn't bother Steve; any personal pride he might once have had was gone. He rarely bathed. What teeth he had left were black and rotting. He wore the same clothing day in and day out. But Jim suspected there was something else going on. For years, he and his wife had cared for her father after a stroke and Jim was intimately aware of how the condition affects both the body and the mind. Steve's lumbering gait, awkward speech, and lack of self-care made him suspect that Steve had also had a stroke.

Steve, however, wasn't looking for friendship. The stroke had hardened his learned tendency toward suspicion into something nearer paranoia. "But underneath," says Jim, "he was screaming for affection." Gradually, Steve began to warm up to Jim and the two developed a friendship of sorts.

"He had a lot of hidden skills," Jim says. Steve's mechanical abilities hadn't been affected and he spent a great deal of time fixing bicycles and tinkering with engines. He loved nothing better than for Jim to come by and ask for help with his truck. Steve would pop the hood, disappear into the depths, muttering and fiddling, and before long the problem was solved.

Jim recognized the vulnerability beneath Steve's brittle exterior; he saw the human being buried deep within the disturbed, dirty, homeless-man shell. Steve had learned to ignore ridicule, fear, and indifference. Charity enraged him. Friendship, however, brought out the best in him. "He was very appreciative," says Jim. "He never forgot a kindness." Jim could see how vital Kitty's affection and companionship were to this man. The most important task in Steve's life was taking care of this small cat, the only creature to depend upon him and stay with him no matter what.

Then one day Steve discovered he was sick. The event he tried to precipitate so many years earlier was threatening to occur from another cause: cancer. The disease simmered slowly at first, but finally Steve could ignore it no longer. He'd managed to keep up his routine, riding his bike around town, collecting bottles, and getting into the occasional fight. "But the cancer was in his spine," says Jim. "He got to where he couldn't walk anymore." Jim got Steve a wheelchair and helped him learn to use it. But one day, Jim wheeled Steve down the grassy path, up to the door of his shack. "Will you be okay now?" Jim asked. Steve nodded and waved his friend away.

That night a vicious rainstorm deluged the valley. In the morning Jim went to check on Steve and found him sitting exactly where he'd left him the day before, soaked to the skin and quaking with cold. He hadn't been able to get himself out of the chair and in through the door. "Why didn't you tell me?" Jim asked in horror. "I didn't want to bother you," answered Steve.

That was it. "You have to go to the hospital," Jim told him. "But what about Kitty?" Steve argued. "Who will take care of Kitty?" Without a plan for his little friend, Steve refused to leave her. So, Jim made arrangements for Kitty to stay at a boarding kennel. Once she was settled in, Jim phoned for an ambulance and reluctantly Steve acquiesced. Although there was little to be done for him, he refused to think of that. He focussed on an improbable future, in which he'd be well enough to join Kitty at home again.

What he didn't know, what he couldn't know, was that Kitty was sick, too.

At first, no one noticed. Many cats stop eating when they're under stress. For the average healthy cat, missing the odd meal or two here and there is of no consequence. Kitty, however, was no longer young and strong. The passing years had left their stamp on her; her slenderness had turned to frailty and her graceful step had become that of a careful old lady. Mild diabetes made it difficult for her to keep weight on. In her peaceful day-to-day routine with Steve, however, her age was barely noticeable.

But suddenly, there was no Steve for Kitty. There was no shack. There was no day-to-day routine anymore. There were only strangers in an unfamiliar place filled with unknown sounds and smells. Being separated from the one person she'd been able to count on and the one stable home she'd known was more than stressful. It was devastating. She stopped eating. She stopped drinking. She simply gave up, getting weaker and weaker each day.

All cats have a powerful instinctive desire to protect themselves from danger by masking signs of illness or injury; Kitty had no one to trust, so she hid her despair. By the time the kennel staff recognized Kitty was starving herself, she was almost beyond hope. The quiet cat who sat motionless at the back of her cage had barely the strength to move. Beneath her once-glossy coat, her slender form had turned to skin and bone. Her luminous eyes had sunk into her skull from dehydration. Fleas had taken advantage of her weakened state, moving in to suck what was left of her lifeblood. Panicking, the caregivers telephoned the nearest veterinary hospital for advice.

"Get her in here, right now!" Dr. Kelly O'Blenis told them. She knew that their only chance of saving Kitty was immediate treatment. When the kennel attendant breathlessly arrived with the tiny bundle, Kelly's heart sank. She scooped up the nearly weightless scrap of fur and gently carried her into the treatment room, calling for help.

Kelly and her assistants did what they could for Kitty, but they had little hope of success. Starvation had sent her diabetes spiralling wildly out of control. Blood loss from the fleas had left her severely anemic. But worst of all was the hopelessness they read in her posture. She was dying before

Steve Perli and Kitty

their eyes, and all of their efforts would be in vain unless she decided to live.

Medical intervention alone could not save this cat, thought Kelly with a familiar stab of frustration. From the tortoiseshell markings to the warm amber eyes, everything about the sad cat hunched in the cage reminded Kelly of Reba, another old cat that had come into her life, several years earlier. Reba ended her life not as a stray, but as a beloved friend, with a home.

Kelly had heard about Steve, and knew he loved Kitty, but the kindhearted veterinarian wondered if the cat felt abandoned. She had the skills to help Kitty get well, but without Steve, it might not be enough. Kitty had a home, and someone who loved her, but she thought she'd lost that. No wonder Kitty had given up.

Kelly steeled herself and telephoned MSA Hospital. Kitty's owner must be told of her condition. She waited while they brought Steve to the phone, drumming her fingers on the counter, dreading the news she had to give him. But Steve surprised her.

"I'll be right there," Steve told her and within the hour, a wheelchair taxi service pulled up to the front of Bakerview Pet Hospital. The driver shouldered open the door and held it while Steve wheeled himself through, hospital gown flapping around his bare ankles. Quickly, they directed him to the cage where his beloved friend lay. He took one look at her and his face crumpled; an anguished sob escaped his lips. He leaned as far into the enclosure as he could from the wheelchair, stroking the still form. As the two met again, both so near the end of their lives, it was as if there was no one else in the room.

"Don't die, baby," he wept. "Don't die!"

Between deep gulping breaths, he began whistling. Softly, in fits and starts, the melody emerged. *Oh Danny boy, the pipes, the pipes are calling.* The barely conscious cat raised her head. *From glen to glen, and down the mountain side.* She pulled herself to her feet, dragging herself nearer the familiar sound. *The summer's gone, and all the flowers are dying.* Steve reached out to her, the tune trembling on his lips. Stumbling weakly, Kitty staggered from the corner of her cage to Steve's hand. *'Tis you, 'tis you must go and I must bide.*

Gently, Steve picked her up and held her closely, his tears flowing into her fur. Kitty collapsed into his familiar arms and for the next hour, the two of them sat together, their ravaged bodies taking refuge in each other's warmth. Kelly tiptoed in and out of the room, trying not to disturb them.

Then suddenly she recognized the melody Steve was whistling and she stood still, listening. "Danny Boy." Could it be? For Dr. Kelly O'Blenis, the Emerald Isle meant far more than shamrocks and St. Patrick's Day parties. Everything from her strawberry blonde hair to her green eyes reflects the Irish in her blood. Nothing Steve did could have affected her more strongly. Several of her co-workers also had to fight back their own tears at the scene playing out before them.

When the time came for Steve to return to his hospital room, he put Kitty back in the cage, stroking her and promising to return tomorrow. The staff assured him that he was welcome to visit as often as he wanted but they could see how difficult it was for him. The excursion had left him pale and exhausted. When the Handi-Dart bus arrived, his hands were shaking and his breathing ragged. He allowed himself to be loaded in, then turned his face to the window and closed his eyes.

When Kelly arrived at the clinic the next morning, she fully expected to learn that Kitty had died in the night. They'd done everything possible for her; they'd given her intravenous fluids to rehydrate her and emergency drugs to counteract the diabetic crisis she had experienced. They'd got rid of the fleas and treated her anemia. They'd offered her small amounts of food, which she had refused. But Kelly knew that Kitty was still critically ill. She steeled herself for bad news.

But Kitty had not died. That morning she'd even eaten a bit of food. A rasping, weak purr greeted anyone attempting to care for her. Within hours, it had become apparent to them all that Kitty's condition had turned a corner. Steve was not gone; that was all she needed to know. She'd decided to live, for Steve.

Just as she had once listened for the sound of a familiar car in the driveway, now she listened for the sound of Steve's voice and the squeak of the motorized wheelchair he now drove. When Steve rolled through the hospital doors, she perked up, waiting for him to come to her cage. Each time, the joy that shone from Steve's face was met with a throaty greeting, as excited as she could be in her emaciated condition. The two sat quietly together during their visits. Sometimes Steve whistled or sang to her; sometimes he picked her up and held her close. With Steve's encouragement, she ate. For Steve, she purred. Mostly, they just took quiet comfort from each other. She had not been abandoned and this, it seemed, was enough for her to fight for life. Day after day, her condition stabilized, her thin frame fleshed out again and the gloss returned to her coat.

During that time, it wasn't uncommon to see Steve on his scooter puttering at full-speed down the street between his hospital and Kitty's hospital. Bare-footed, his thin hospital gown flapping up around his thighs in the wind, he attracted a lot of attention. The police, who had got to know Steve well over the years, stopped him after distraught motorists called to alert them that someone had "escaped" from the hospital. Steve couldn't have cared less what kind of spectacle he made. He lived for his visitation time with Kitty and nothing short of death would stop him.

But death would stop him. Now Steve had a difficult decision to make. Although Kitty was well enough to go home, Steve was not, and never would be. The doctors had been clear: his time on earth was short. He'd long ago made peace with his mortality, but how could he leave Kitty? He agonized over what would become of his beloved cat. The chances of anyone wanting to adopt such an elderly, frail cat were slim. And even if someone did, Kitty didn't want to get to know a new family.

Because there was nowhere to send Kitty home to, Kelly delayed discharging her. It wasn't as if the cat couldn't still benefit from veterinary care, she rationalized. One week passed, then another. Every morning Kitty greeted the staff as they brought meals to the hospitalized patients and cleaned their cages. "We'll just keep her one more day," Kelly said each time, knowing that as long as he could, Steve would keep coming to see her. Who could say which one of them got more out of the visits?

As Kitty became familiar with the sounds and smells of the animal hospital, and as she watched Steve interact with Kelly and the other staff members, she grew more comfortable. She began chirping plaintively at the staff member on morning kennel duty, begging for a little time to stretch her legs. Kelly looked the other way when the staff began allowing Kitty to wander around the treatment room while they worked. She bothered no one, contentedly tiptoeing in and out of corners, exploring this new and interesting territory. Then Kelly began letting Kitty sit with her while she ate her lunch.

The first time Steve was unable to keep his visitation date with Kitty, everyone felt so badly for her that they lavished her with special attention. They knew they could not take Steve's place, but they had to do what they could to comfort her. Kelly had to make a decision. She could no longer allow Kitty to stay in the clinic. The cage she occupied could at any time be needed for a patient, but not only that, the germs carried in by sick animals were too dangerous for her. But Kelly couldn't bear to relinquish the gentle old cat to a shelter. Kitty needed a quiet home with someone she trusted, for the little time she had left. Kelly knew what she had to do. She would take Kitty home with her. This old, fragile cat, who looked so much like Reba, deserved to end her days in whatever comfort she could find.

Within hours of arriving at Kelly's home, Kitty discovered a hitherto unknown delight: the fireplace. She quickly found a favourite spot on the hearth and spent hour after hour warming her old bones in the soft, flickering light.

Heavy medication gave Steve relief from the cancer pain that ravaged his body, but when he was conscious, his only thought was for Kitty. When he learned she had gone to live with Kelly, his entire body sagged with relief. He was barely able to acknowledge the news, but it was clear to Jim that the final worry of his life had been lifted. With Kitty's future assured, Steve agreed to move to the palliative care centre. "Knowing that Kelly was taking Kitty put Steve at rest," says Jim. Two days later, Steve passed from this life.

Kelly diligently checked Kitty's blood sugar levels and gave her insulin as needed, but Kitty's condition had improved so dramatically she needed little medical care. Nevertheless, when Kelly came home one day, only a few weeks after Steve's death, and found Kitty peacefully curled up by the fire, she knew that it was not the stillness of sleep she was seeing. No ear flicked at the slam of the door. No murky-eyed head lifted in greeting. The old cat had at last followed her beloved friend into the next world.

Since that fateful meeting so long ago, not one day went by when Steve and Kitty were not together, but up until his death, memories of that dark time in his life remained fresh enough to draw tears. One little animal had changed the course of his life. Kitty, he believed, had given him back his life and made it worth living.

After all they've been through together, it's hard not to believe that somehow, somewhere, Steve and Kitty will find each other again. All he has to do is whistle and his Kitty will come running.

Oh Danny boy, the pipes, the pipes are calling
From glen to glen, and down the mountain side.
The summer's gone, and all the flowers are dying.
'Tis you, 'tis you must go, and I must bide.

But come ye back when summer's in the meadow
Or when the valley's hushed and white with snow,
'Tis I'll be there, in sunshine or in shadow.
Oh Danny boy, oh Danny boy, I love you so.

But if you come when all the flowers are dying
And I am dead, as dead I well may be,
Ye'll come and find the place where I am lying
And kneel, and say an "Ave" there for me.

And I shall hear, tho' soft you tread above me,
And all my dreams will warmer, sweeter be.
If you'll not fail to tell me that you love me,
I'll simply sleep in peace until you come to me.

Epilogue

ONE STEAMY AUGUST MORNING, LONG after Cinders and Nutmeg had crossed into misty memory, I stepped out into the shaded backyard, craving, like many another busy mother, an hour of solitude. There, in the corner crouched an unfamiliar cat. A strikingly beautiful, frightened-looking calico.

She was the most gorgeous three-coloured cat I'd ever seen. Her face was half black, half orange, like Nutmeg's had been, but she had the tortoiseshell markings and thin stripe down her nose, like Cinders. The fur on her tail was four inches long and the colours blended together to form a rich dark chocolate-caramel swirl. She danced just out of reach for a few minutes, then gave in to my cajoling, voicing her anxiety and desperation in a stuttering, chirping mew.

She arched her back against my hand. The body that pushed into my fingers was alarmingly thin, the bones jutting out from the skin. Just then, my three daughters came outside and we set to work getting her cool water, shade, and a decent meal. From behind the windows, our resident cats watched, hissing and growling.

The next morning the backyard was empty. But, two days later, during a summer rainstorm, the stray reappeared, alone and hungry as ever. I pulled a plastic patio-chair up against the house where it was dry. This time, she didn't leave. Each morning when I opened the blinds, there she was, yawning and stretching and reaching for me.

We did what we could to find her home, but no one responded to our notices. Finally, after three weeks, a choice had to be made. She either had to go to the pound, or we had to adopt her.

We named her Sophie.

She walked into our home as if she'd been waiting all her life for just such a moment. Tabitha watched in high dudgeon from her perch atop the cat tree. Mylos hissed and snarled from a corner of the room, then disappeared in a fit of pique. Cody, our old boy, peeked through the banister rails, only the twitch of his tail betraying his annoyance.

Sophie watched them all calmly, then sat down and began washing herself. She presented no threat, but nor would she recognize their rejection. Finally, they began to recover their dignity, stalking stiffly past Sophie as if she weren't there. Within a few weeks, she'd been incorporated into our little feline circle.

Why did she pick us? Probably half the people on our street would have offered her shelter. Maybe we were simply the first. Maybe she stayed because we fed her. Maybe, as folklore says, she has the ability of three-coloured cats to see into the future and that future featured us. Whatever the reason, serendipity sent Sophie to our home. Has she brought us luck? I couldn't say. But I do know this: here I sit, writing a book of cat stories. How lucky is that?

Acknowledgements

The author would like to thank the many people who generously shared their cat stories with her: Alexandria, Joyce and Dale Tiffinger, Edith Donnelly, Cathie Newman, Joyce Smith, Danielle Allen, Catherine Hamm, Michelle Shaw, Dave Hargreaves, Davena Tarkanen, Garth Ukrainetz, and Jim Matthies. A special thanks to Dr. Kelly O'Blenis and all the staff at Bakerview Pet Hospital.